microwaving for one & two

microwave cooking library™

by barbara methven

microwave cooking library™

According to the last census, there are more households of one or two people than ever before in history. Their number is growing. The microwave oven is an ideal appliance for the small household. Savings in time and energy can be dramatic. Many foods can be mixed, cooked and eaten from a single casserole.

Most microwave cookbooks, however, are written for four to six servings; cutting yields results in complicated measurements and new cooking times. *Microwaving for One & Two* is tailored to the small household. Most of the recipes are written for one serving with complete directions for preparing two. Some recipes yield two servings because the food cannot be prepared in a smaller amount. Instructions are provided for storing and reheating the second serving. There are recipes for mini cakes, breads, and pies. Special sections show you how to make the most of large cuts of meat when they are available at a special price, without tiresome leftovers; how to use large vegetables or a one-layer cake mix.

The recipes are designed to keep measurement simple and avoid leftover ingredients. Since a full can of some foods, like tomato paste, would be too much for one or two servings, a unique chart tells you how to store these foods and lists all the recipes where they can be used.

With your microwave oven and the variety of recipes offered here, creative cooking for one or two can be fast, simple and intriguing.

Barbara Methven

Barbara Methven

CREDITS:

Design & Production: Cy DeCosse Creative Department, Inc.
Consultant: Joanne Crocker
Art Director: Delores Swanson
Production Coordinators: Mary Ann Knox, Christine Watkins, Elizabeth Woods, Bonita Machel
Photographers: Buck Holzemer, Jill Greer, Ken Greer
Food Stylists: Lynn Lohmann, Susan Zechmann, Suzanne Finley
Home Economists: Peggy Lamb, Jill Crum, Kathy Webber
Typesetting: Ellen Sorenson
Color Separations: Weston Engraving Co., Inc.
Printing: Moebius Printing Co.

Additional volumes in the Microwave Cooking Library series are available from the publisher:

• Basic Microwaving
• Recipe Conversion for Microwave
• Microwaving Meats
• Microwave Baking & Desserts
• Microwaving Meals in 30 Minutes
• Microwaving on a Diet
• Microwaving Fruits & Vegetables
• Microwaving Convenience Foods
• Microwaving for Holidays & Parties
• The Microwave & Freezer

Contents

What You Need to Know Before You Start

Cooking for one and two begins in the supermarket. As the average family size decreases, grocery stores are catering more to the needs of the smaller household.

Many supermarkets and co-op groceries allow you to hand-pick loose produce, so you can buy a handful of green beans, rather than a pre-packaged pound, or select one tomato rather than taking several in a sealed tray.

If your market doesn't have a butcher behind the counter, learn to ring the bell for service and request just one pork chop or one-quarter pound of ground beef as you need it.

Buying for one or two has advantages. For a special occasion, tenderloin steak or a rack of lamb costs less than dinner out. The cook who must feed four to six people may find the cost of steak or seafood prohibitive, no matter how special the occasion.

Some cuts of meat aren't available in small sizes. If you crave pot roast or want to take advantage of a special on pork loins, you don't have to cook the whole piece and eat leftovers for days. This book shows you how to divide larger cuts to make several different recipes. There are similar directions for using a one-layer cake mix and a head of cauliflower, and an acorn squash.

You can buy one-half dozen eggs and one stick of butter. Keep bread in the freezer and remove slices as needed.

A good variety of food is available in small can sizes. The small cans may cost a little more per ounce, but the large economy size is false economy if you end up refrigerating leftovers and throwing them out after a few days.

When you buy frozen vegetables, bigger is better for the small household. You can open a poly bag of loose pack vegetables, remove what you need, and reclose the bag with a twist tie. That's easier than dividing a solid block of vegetables and trying to reseal the box.

How to Use This Book

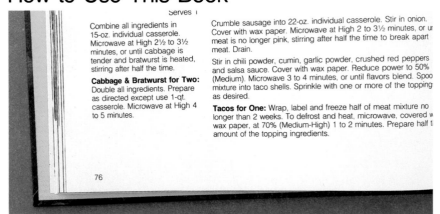

Serves 1

Combine all ingredients in 15-oz. individual casserole. Microwave at High 2½ to 3½ minutes, or until cabbage is tender and bratwurst is heated, stirring after half the time.

Cabbage & Bratwurst for Two: Double all ingredients. Prepare as directed except use 1-qt. casserole. Microwave at High 4 to 5 minutes.

Crumble sausage into 22-oz. individual casserole. Stir in onion. Cover with wax paper. Microwave at High 2 to 3½ minutes, or until meat is no longer pink, stirring after half the time to break apart meat. Drain.

Stir in chili powder, cumin, garlic powder, crushed red peppers and salsa sauce. Cover with wax paper. Reduce power to 50% (Medium). Microwave 3 to 4 minutes, or until flavors blend. Spoon mixture into taco shells. Sprinkle with one or more of the topping as desired.

Tacos for One: Wrap, label and freeze half of meat mixture no longer than 2 weeks. To defrost and heat, microwave, covered with wax paper, at 70% (Medium-High) 1 to 2 minutes. Prepare half the amount of the topping ingredients.

76

Where possible, the recipes in this book are formulated for one serving. If you're cooking for two, directions at the end of the recipe tell you how to double the recipe and increase microwaving time. Some ingredients can not be doubled. Because of the increased cooking time, the same amount of seasoning may be enough to flavor the food. In some recipes, the cooking time doesn't change. If the food needs time to tenderize or develop flavor, one portion may take the same time as two.

Recipes which are written for two servings cannot be cut in half. They will not work in smaller amounts. If you are cooking for one, directions at the end of the recipe tell you how to store and reheat the second serving. Maximum storage times are also included.

Utensils

The right utensils are needed when you're cooking for one or two. A small amount of food does not microwave properly if it is spread thinly in a large casserole. You don't have to re-equip your kitchen; this book uses many standard utensils found in larger households. However, you will want to invest in a few inexpensive, small dishes. Many of them can be used for cooking, serving and storing.

Size is important. The 12-, 14- and 15-oz. individual casseroles cook and serve single servings, while the 22-oz. casserole serves two. Don't substitute a smaller casserole, even if the food fits. The greater depth is needed to contain boiling or permit stirring.

Special sizes you will use often are the 6½×4-in. loaf dish, 7-in. pie plate, and a 10×6-in. baking dish which can be fitted with a small roasting rack.

Covers of glass for microwaving are provided with many individual casseroles. Soft plastic covers are useful for storage, but should not be used for cooking. Substitute plastic wrap.

Compare bottom dimensions if you want to substitute a larger casserole for the one recommended in a recipe. You may use a casserole with deeper sides if the bottom surface is the same. The meat loaf fits in any of the three dishes on the left; the casserole fits in either of the two dishes on the right.

Shapes accommodate different food shapes. Both these casseroles hold 14 ounces, but are not interchangeable because of the shape or depth of food.

Standard equipment you may already have includes custard and measuring cups, 1- and 2-qt. glass or pyroceram casseroles, 8 × 8-in. baking dishes, coffee mugs and 15-oz. soup bowls.

Additional special sizes for the small household are a 6½-in. pyroceram skillet with glass cover, 2½-cup ring dish and small browning dish.

Freezing Food for One & Two

The storage life of frozen foods depends on the temperature of your freezer. Chest freezers maintain an optimum temperature of 0°F. or lower, but few small households have this type of freezer. Usually, the temperature in a combination refrigerator-freezer with double doors is above 0°F. The freezer compartment of a single door refrigerator is about 15° to 18°F. Freezer storage charts in this book are based on the two-door combination. If you have a freezer compartment, use the food within the recommended time for best quality. Food is safe after the recommended freezer limit, but flavor and texture are lost.

Packaging also affects the quality of frozen foods. It is important to eliminate as much air as possible from the package before freezing. Use a moisture-proof, vapor-proof plastic wrap, freezer wrap or heavy duty foil. Air leaches moisture from food and produces freezer burn, which destroys the flavor and texture of food. Before freezing meat, trim excess fat. Fat may develop a rancid flavor when frozen beyond recommended storage times.

Tips for Freezing

Freeze food in single portions even if you are cooking for two. Wrap individually or loose-pack. Single portions are easier to use and defrost uniformly.

Separate chops or burgers with a double layer of freezer wrap or plastic wrap if you wish to stack them and wrap them all in one package.

Label all packages with the type of food, amount or portion size, and date. Use within the recommended time.

How to Loose-Pack

Spread small items like vegetable cuts, ¼-lb. portions of ground beef or individual chops on baking sheet.

Freeze until firm. Remove from baking sheet and place in heavy-duty plastic freezer bag.

Squeeze out as much air as possible. Seal with twist tie. To use, remove desired portions; re-seal bag and return to freezer.

How to Package in Plastic Bags

Use heat-sealable or heavy-duty freezer bags. Place food in bag.

Press out as much air as possible. Seal bag with heat-sealer or reclosable twist ties. Label with moisture-proof marker.

How to Wrap with Aluminum Foil or Freezer Paper

Cut off enough wrap to go around meat 1½ times. Bring edges of wrap together and fold over 1 inch.

Fold again. Press wrap tightly against meat to force out as much air as possible.

Crease ends of wrap to form triangles. Fold up, molding tightly around meat. Seal with continuous strip of freezer tape.

How to Freeze Casseroles

Line dish with foil or plastic wrap. Place food in dish. Freeze.

Remove frozen food from dish. Wrap tightly with foil or freezer paper, pressing out air. Store in freezer. Dish is free for other uses.

To serve, unwrap food and return to dish. Defrosting and heating times in this book are for frozen food in room temperature dish. If dish is cold, additional time will be needed.

What to Do With Leftover Ingredients

The recipes in this book have been designed to avoid leftover ingredients. In some cases, however, a food may not be available in small quantities, or the entire amount would be too strong in flavor for one or two servings, so you'll have leftover ingredients. In most cases, extra canned foods can be refrigerated in the original can, tightly covered with foil. Fresh items should be stored in plastic wrap or bag. The chart below lists recipes which call for these foods so you can plan to use leftover ingredients within the recommended storage time.

Leftover Ingredient Storage Chart

Item	Maximum Storage Time	Other Suggested Uses
Applesauce	Refrigerator: 1 week	Applesauce Squash, page 119 Gingered Applesauce Bread, page 135
Black Olives	Refrigerator: 4 weeks	Mexican Egg Casserole, page 110 Tostada, page 27 Vegetable Enchiladas, page 129
Crab Meat	Refrigerator: 2 days	Stuffed Shrimp, page 104 Spinach-Stuffed Sole, page 102
Cranberry Sauce	Refrigerator: 1 week	Cranberry-Apple Glazed Cornish Hen, page 96
Cream Cheese	Refrigerator: 2 weeks	Artichoke Mustard Dip, page 127 Spinach-Stuffed Sole, page 102
Eggs, Whole Beaten	Refrigerator: 4 weeks Refrigerator: 4 days Freezer: 4 months*	
Green Chilies	Refrigerator: 3 days Freezer: 2 weeks*	Mexican Egg Casserole, page 110 Tamales, page 60 Chicken Avocado Salad, page 88 Vegetable Enchiladas, page 129
Green Pepper Chopped	Refrigerator: 3 to 5 days Freezer: 3 months	
Onion Chopped	Refrigerator: 3 to 5 days Freezer: 3 months	
Pineapple	Refrigerator: 1 week	Ham Loaf, page 66 Fruited Slaw, page 126
Tomato Fresh	Refrigerator: 3 days	Marinated Cauliflower Salad, page 123 Mexican Pizza, page 13
Tomato Paste	Refrigerator: 5 days Freezer: 2 weeks*	Lasagna Rolls, page 48 Chili, page 46 Mostaccioli & Meat Sauce, page 77
Water Chestnuts	Refrigerator: 3 days	Seafood Kabobs, page 14 Pork Chow Mein, page 58

*To defrost:

Eggs: Microwave one-half of beaten egg (1 tablespoon plus 1½ teaspoon) at 10% (Low) 2½ to 6 minutes, stirring after half the time. Let stand to complete defrosting.

Green Chilies: Microwave one-half can (4 oz.) at 50% (Medium) 45 seconds to 1½ minutes, stirring to break apart after half the time.

Tomato Paste: Microwave at 50% (Medium) 15 to 60 seconds, scraping off defrosted portions every 15 seconds. Return any unused portions to freezer.

Storage Tips

Check expiration dates on dry foods, like cereals and mixes, bottled sauces and dressings, and dairy products.

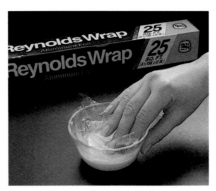

Beaten egg. Freeze in small glass or plastic containers. Place plastic wrap directly on egg surface. Cover dish with foil. Do not refreeze.

Green pepper and onions. Seed pepper or peel onion. Wash and chop. Loose-pack as directed on page 8.

Water chestnuts. Drain liquid. Cover chestnuts with fresh water. Refrigerate. Change water daily.

Tomato paste and green chilies or jalapeño peppers. Remove to airtight glass jar. Refrigerate or freeze.

Black olives. Remove to glass jar, if desired. Make sure all of the olives are covered with liquid. Refrigerate.

Recipe Conversion

The recipes in this book are already cut to the smallest amounts possible, but you may have other large recipes you'd like to adapt to a smaller size. These measurement charts will aid you in dividing standard measurements. As a guide to microwaving time, use a recipe in this book for a similar amount and type of food.

Equivalent Measurements

    1 tablespoon = 3 teaspoons
          1 cup = 16 tablespoons = 8 ounces
        ¼ cup = 4 tablespoons
        ⅓ cup = 5 tablespoons plus 1 teaspoon
        1 pint = 2 cups = 16 ounces
       1 quart = 4 cups (2 pints) = 32 ounces
      1 pound = 16 ounces
     ½ pound = 8 ounces
     ¼ pound = 4 ounces

Dividing Measurements

Measurement	Half of Measurement
⅛ teaspoon	Dash
1 tablespoon	1½ teaspoons
¼ cup	2 tablespoons
⅓ cup	2 tablespoons plus 2 teaspoons
¾ cup	6 tablespoons

Appetizers

Appetizers can serve as a light meal, or make an occasion of an everyday dinner. Many of these recipes can be made in advance and enjoyed while you microwave the main dish.

◄ Mexican Pizza

¼ lb. lean ground beef
¼ cup chopped onion
¼ teaspoon chili powder
⅛ teaspoon dried oregano
    leaves
⅛ teaspoon ground cumin
⅛ teaspoon garlic salt
¼ cup chopped tomato
 1 flour tortilla, 10-in. diameter
¼ cup chopped green pepper
½ cup shredded Monterey Jack
    cheese
½ cup shredded Cheddar
    cheese

Serves 2

Place ground beef and onion in 1-qt. casserole. Microwave at High 1 to 1½ minutes, or until meat is no longer pink, stirring after half the time to break apart. Drain. Stir in chili powder, oregano, cumin and garlic salt. Reduce power to 50% (Medium). Microwave 2 to 3 minutes, or until flavors blend. Stir in tomato.

Increase power to High. Preheat microwave pizza stone 6 minutes, or pyroceram pizza browner 5 minutes. Assemble pizza by sprinkling meat mixture over tortilla. Add green pepper and Monterey Jack and Cheddar cheese. Transfer pizza carefully to preheated stone or browner.

Microwave at High 2 to 3 minutes, or until cheese is melted and bubbly. Remove from stone to slice. If desired, garnish with shredded lettuce and serve with salsa or taco sauce.

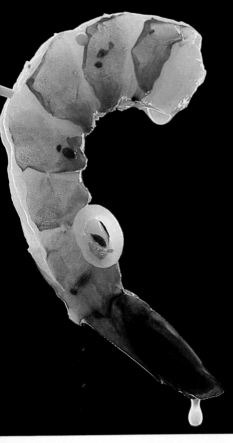

◄ Pickled Shrimp

½ cup beer
1 bay leaf
1 teaspoon whole, mixed pickling spice
1 small onion, thinly sliced
½ teaspoon whole peppercorns
½ teaspoon salt
½ lb. fresh, raw colossal shrimp, shelled and deveined

Serves 2

Combine all ingredients except shrimp in 1-qt. casserole; cover. Microwave at High 2 to 3 minutes, or until boiling. Remove cover. Microwave at High 1 minute. Stir in shrimp; cover. Reduce power to 50% (Medium). Microwave 2½ to 3 minutes, or until shrimp are opaque, stirring after half the time. Refrigerate no longer than 2 days. Serve cold.

Sautéed Mushrooms

3 tablespoons butter or margarine
1 tablespoon finely chopped onion
1 small clove garlic, minced
3 cups fresh mushrooms, cut in half
¼ teaspoon salt
⅛ teaspoon pepper

Serves 2

Place butter, onion and garlic in 1-qt. casserole. Microwave at High 2 to 3 minutes, or until butter melts and onion and garlic begin to brown, stirring after half the time.

Add mushrooms, salt and pepper; stir to coat. Cover with wax paper. Microwave at High 1½ to 3 minutes, or until tender, stirring after half the time.

◄ Seafood Kabobs

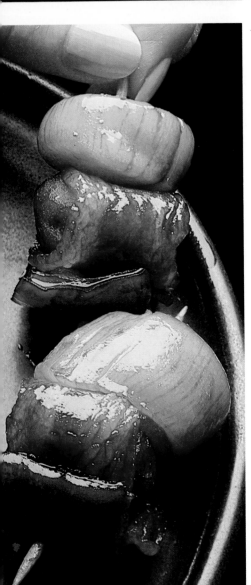

1 slice bacon, cut into thirds
1 tablespoon plus 1½ teaspoons soy sauce
1 tablespoon honey
1½ teaspoons white wine
⅛ teaspoon ground ginger

Dash garlic powder
3 whole water chestnuts
3 scallops
¼ medium green pepper, cut into 3 pieces, 1 × 1-in.

Serves 1

Place bacon pieces in 1-qt. casserole. Microwave at High 30 to 45 seconds, or until partially cooked. Drain on paper towel. Discard all but ½ teaspoon bacon fat. Stir soy sauce, honey, wine, ginger and garlic powder into fat in casserole. Microwave at High 1 to 2 minutes, or until honey dissolves, stirring after half the time.

Wrap water chestnuts in bacon pieces. Assemble kabobs by placing one scallop, one bacon-wrapped water chestnut and one green pepper chunk on each of three wooden picks. Place kabobs in soy-honey mixture, turning to coat. Cover and refrigerate 2 hours, turning kabobs over after half the time.

Arrange kabobs on roasting rack with scallops to outer edge. Microwave at High 1 to 2 minutes, or until scallops are opaque and flake easily, turning over and basting with marinade after half the time.

Seafood Kabobs for Two: Double all ingredients. Prepare as directed except microwave bacon 45 to 60 seconds and reserve 1 teaspoon fat. Microwave kabobs 2 to 3 minutes.

Chicken Wing Drumsticks

2 chicken wings*
1½ teaspoons butter or margarine
3 tablespoons corn flake crumbs
2 teaspoons grated Parmesan cheese
⅛ teaspoon dried basil leaves
⅛ teaspoon paprika
Dash salt
Dash garlic powder

Serves 1

*If frozen, microwave two chicken wings at 50% (Medium) 1 to 2 minutes or four chicken wings 2½ minutes, or until defrosted, turning over and rearranging after half the time.

Chicken Wing Drumsticks for Two: Double all ingredients. Prepare as directed except microwave 2 to 3 minutes.

How to Microwave Chicken Wing Drumsticks

Cut each chicken wing at joint to make two pieces. Wing tip end can be frozen no longer than 2 weeks. Use in Chicken Soup & Dumplings, page 21.

Loosen meat and skin from narrow end of bone.

Push meat and skin down towards large end of bone, pulling over end of bone to form a ball. Set aside.

Place butter in small bowl. Microwave at High 30 to 45 seconds, or until melted. Mix remaining ingredients in another bowl.

Dip meaty end of chicken wing in melted butter. Roll in crumb mixture to coat. Arrange on microwave roasting rack with meaty portion to outer edge.

Cover with wax paper. Microwave at High 1 to 1½ minutes, or until meat is no longer pink and juices run clear, rearranging after half the time.

15

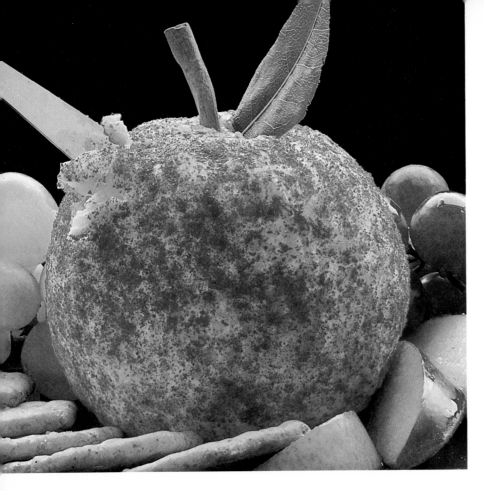

Port Wine Cheese Ball ▲

1 pkg. (3 oz.) cream cheese
1½ cups grated sharp Cheddar
 cheese
3 teaspoons port wine
 Paprika
1 stick cinnamon
1 bay leaf

Makes 1 cheese ball

Place cream cheese in medium
bowl. Microwave at 50% (Medium) 30 to 60 seconds, or until
softened. Blend in Cheddar
cheese and port wine. Shape
into ball.

Wrap in wax paper or plastic
wrap. Chill until slightly set,
about 1 hour. Form into apple
shape. Sprinkle with paprika.
Use cinnamon stick for stem
and bay leaf for leaf. Serve with
crackers, apple and pear slices,
or grape clusters, if desired.
Refrigerate, wrapped, no longer
than 2 weeks.

Barbecued Meatballs

¼ lb. ground beef
1 tablespoon seasoned bread
 crumbs
½ teaspoon dried parsley flakes
½ teaspoon dried minced onion
⅛ teaspoon salt
⅛ teaspoon pepper
½ teaspoon lemon juice
½ cup barbecue sauce, divided

Serves 2

In small bowl mix ground beef,
bread crumbs, parsley flakes,
minced onion, salt, pepper,
lemon juice and 2 teaspoons
barbecue sauce. Shape by
heaping teaspoonfuls into 10
meatballs. Place in 6¾ × 4½-in.
dish. Add remaining barbecue
sauce. Cover with wax paper.
Microwave at High 2 to 3½
minutes, or until meatballs are
firm and no longer pink, stirring
sauce and rearranging meatballs after half the time. Skim fat
before serving. Refrigerate
leftover meatballs no longer
than 2 days.

Bacon & Horseradish Dip

Pictured opposite, top left

1 slice bacon
1 pkg. (3 oz.) cream cheese
1 tablespoon yogurt or dairy
 sour cream
2 teaspoons horseradish
1 green onion, chopped

Makes ⅓ cup

Place bacon on paper towel-
lined plate. Microwave at High 1
to 1½ minutes, or until brown.
Crumble. Place cream cheese
in 10-oz. custard cup. Reduce
power to 50% (Medium). Microwave 30 to 60 seconds, or until
softened. Blend in yogurt,
horseradish and green onion.
Sprinkle with bacon. Refrigerate
no longer than 2 days.

Onion Dip

Pictured opposite, top right

1 pkg. (3 oz.) cream cheese
1 tablespoon yogurt or dairy
 sour cream
½ teaspoon dried onion flakes
¼ teaspoon instant beef
 bouillon granules
1 teaspoon water
¼ teaspoon Worcestershire
 sauce
1 tablespoon chopped walnuts
 or pecans

Makes ⅓ cup

Place cream cheese in 10-oz.
custard cup or small bowl.
Microwave at 50% (Medium) 30
to 60 seconds, or until softened.
Blend in yogurt. In 6-oz. custard
cup mix onion flakes, bouillon
granules and water. Cover with
plastic wrap. Increase power to
High. Microwave 30 seconds,
stirring to dissolve bouillon. Stir
into cream cheese mixture. Add
Worcestershire sauce. Sprinkle
with chopped nuts. Serve hot or
cold with chips, or celery and
carrot sticks, if desired. Refrigerate dip no longer than 2 days.

Variation:
Chili Dip: Substitute 1 tablespoon chili sauce and ⅛ teaspoon chili powder for onion
flakes, bouillon granules, water,
Worcestershire sauce and nuts.

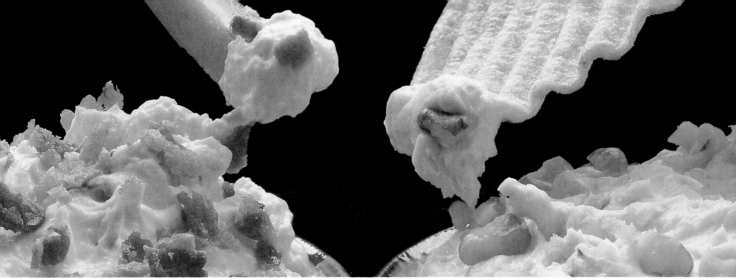

Marinated Vegetables ►

2 cups white vinegar
⅓ cup sugar
1½ teaspoons salt
5 medium carrots, peeled and
    cut into julienne strips,
    2 × ¼-in.
1½ cups fresh broccoli
    flowerets and ¼-in.
    stem slices
1 cup fresh cauliflowerets
2 green pepper rings,
    ½-in. thick
½ cup water
2 whole cloves garlic
1 tablespoon vegetable oil,
    divided

Makes 2 pints

In 4-cup measure mix vinegar, sugar and salt. Cover with plastic wrap. Microwave at High 4 to 6 minutes, or until mixture begins to boil. Boil 1 minute. Cool. Place carrots, broccoli, cauliflowerets, green pepper and water in 2-qt. casserole; cover. Microwave at High 3 to 4 minutes, or until vegetables are vibrant colors but still crisp, stirring after half the time. Drain and rinse under cold water.

Layer vegetables in two 1-pint jars as follows: stand carrots upright, add green pepper ring, layer of cauliflowerets and broccoli, then clove of garlic. Pour half of vinegar mixture into each jar. Add 1½ teaspoons oil to each; cover. Refrigerate at least 5 days before serving and no longer than 4 weeks.

Beverages

These tangy or sweet beverages include make-ahead mixes to serve steaming hot. For cool refreshment, try fruit cubes in a carbonated beverage.

◄ Banana Cooler

½ cup sugar
1 cup water
1 banana, mashed
¾ cup orange juice
¼ cup pineapple juice
2 tablespoons lemon juice

Makes 14 cubes

In 4-cup measure combine sugar and water. Microwave at High 3 to 5 minutes, or until boiling. Continue to microwave 1 minute. Blend in remaining ingredients. Pour into 14-cube ice tray; freeze 4 hours. Store in plastic freezer bag.

For each serving: Place two cubes in 8-oz. glass. Pour ginger ale, lemon-lime soda, orange soda or carbonated water over cubes.

Citrus Tea Mix

1 cup orange-flavored instant breakfast drink powder
¾ cup instant tea powder
½ cup pre-sweetened lemon-flavored drink mix
¼ cup powdered sugar
½ teaspoon ground cinnamon
¼ teaspoon ground cloves

Makes 2½ cups

In 1-qt. bowl or jar mix all ingredients. Place in airtight container and date. Store no longer than 6 months.

For each serving: Microwave ¾ cup hot water at High 1 to 2 minutes, or until boiling. Blend in 2 tablespoons Citrus Tea Mix. Garnish with lemon or orange slices, if desired.

Hot Buttered Lemonade ▲

1 cup water
  Juice of 1 lemon
3 tablespoons honey
2 sticks cinnamon
2 tablespoons dark rum,
  optional
2 teaspoons butter or margarine

Serves 2

In 4-cup measure combine water, lemon juice, honey and cinnamon sticks. Microwave at High 3½ to 4½ minutes, or until boiling, stirring once after half the time. Stir in rum. Garnish each serving with 1 teaspoon butter. Stir with cinnamon sticks.

Variation:

Hot Limeade: In 4-cup measure combine 1 cup water, juice of 1 lime and 3 tablespoons sugar. Prepare as directed. Add 2 tablespoons light rum and 1 drop green food coloring. Garnish with fresh strawberries or lemon or lime slices, if desired.

Hot Chocolate Mix

  3 cups non-fat dry milk
    powder
1½ cups powdered sugar
  ⅓ cup plus 1 tablespoon cocoa
  ⅓ cup non-dairy creamer
    Dash salt

Makes 5 cups

In 1½- to 2-qt. bowl or jar mix all ingredients. Place in airtight container and date. Store no longer than 6 months.

For each serving: Microwave ¾ cup hot water at High 1 to 2 minutes, or until boiling. Blend in ¼ cup Hot Chocolate Mix.

Variations:

Spicy Hot Chocolate: Blend dash of ground cinnamon and ground nutmeg into one serving prepared hot chocolate. Garnish with a cinnamon stick.

Hot Mocha: Blend ¼ teaspoon instant coffee granules into one serving prepared hot chocolate. Garnish with Whipped Cream, page 151.

Hot Vegetable Drink ▲

1 cup water
1 cup shredded cabbage,
  page 124
1 large carrot, cut lengthwise in
  half, then into 2-in. pieces
1 stalk celery, cut lengthwise in
  half, then into 2-in. pieces
1 small onion, thinly sliced
1 clove garlic
1 cup tomato juice
1 or 2 drops red pepper sauce
  Dash coarse ground pepper

Serves 2

In 1-qt. casserole combine water, cabbage, carrot, celery, onion and garlic; cover. Microwave at High 13 to 17 minutes, or until vegetables are very tender, stirring twice during cooking. Remove vegetables from broth. Stir remaining ingredients into broth. Cover. Microwave at High 2 to 3 minutes, or until desired serving temperature. Garnish each serving with cucumber or zucchini spear, if desired.

19

Soups

Homemade soups don't have to be made in stockpot quantities or simmered for hours. These intriguing soups microwave in minutes, have a delightful fresh flavor and make just enough for one or two servings.

◀ Chicken Soup & Dumplings

Soup:
  1 lb. broiler-fryer chicken
      pieces (breasts, wings
      or legs)
  2 cups water
  1 carrot, sliced
  1 stalk celery, sliced
  1 teaspoon salt
  ⅛ teaspoon dried savory leaves

Dumplings:
  ½ cup all-purpose flour
  ½ teaspoon baking powder
  ¼ teaspoon dried parsley flakes
  ¼ teaspoon salt
  2 tablespoons milk
  1 egg

Serves 2

In 1½- to 2-qt. casserole combine chicken pieces, water, carrot, celery, salt and savory; cover. Microwave at High 18 to 20 minutes, or until chicken is no longer pink, turning pieces over and stirring broth 2 or 3 times during cooking. Skim fat. Remove chicken. Skin and bone chicken; cut into pieces. Return to soup; cover and set aside. In small bowl blend dumpling ingredients well. Drop by teaspoonfuls onto soup; cover. Microwave at High 2 to 3 minutes, or until dumplings are light and springy to the touch and no longer doughy.

Chicken Soup & Dumplings for One: Refrigerate one serving no longer than 2 days. To reheat, microwave, covered, at 50% (Medium) 5 to 8 minutes.

Hot & Sour Soup ▲

½ medium chicken breast,
  about ¼ lb.
2 cups hot water
1 carrot, cut lengthwise in half,
  then into 3-in. pieces
1 stalk celery, cut lengthwise in
  half, then into 3-in. pieces
1 teaspoon salt
½ cup sliced fresh mushrooms
1 tablespoon cornstarch

½ teaspoon white pepper
1 tablespoon white wine
  vinegar
2 teaspoons soy sauce
½ teaspoon sesame oil or
  vegetable oil
1 egg, slightly beaten
1 green onion, cut into thin,
  diagonal pieces

Serves 2

In 1½-qt. casserole combine chicken, water, carrot, celery and
salt; cover. Microwave at High 8 to 10 minutes, or until chicken is
no longer pink, turning meat over and stirring broth after half the
time. Remove chicken and vegetables; reserve broth. Cool
chicken; discard vegetables.

Skin and bone chicken; cut into matchstick pieces. Add chicken
and mushrooms to broth. Microwave at High 4 to 6 minutes, or
until boiling. Mix cornstarch, white pepper, vinegar, soy sauce and
sesame oil; stir into broth. Microwave at High 1 to 2 minutes, or
until slightly thickened, stirring after half the time. Stir soup. Pour
beaten egg in thin stream into soup, stirring in a circular motion.
Sprinkle with green onion pieces.

Hot & Sour Soup for One: Refrigerate one serving no longer than
2 days. To reheat, microwave at 50% (Medium) 5 to 6 minutes,
stirring once or twice.

Cherry Soup

1 can (16 oz.) pitted red tart
  cherries, divided
¼ cup packed brown sugar
1 tablespoon cornstarch
⅛ teaspoon ground nutmeg
¼ cup orange juice

Serves 2

Place undrained cherries in
1-qt. casserole. Remove six
cherries; set aside. Mix brown
sugar, cornstarch, nutmeg and
orange juice. Stir into cherries in
casserole. Microwave at High 4
to 5 minutes, or until clear and
thickened, stirring 2 or 3 times.

Press through strainer. Discard
pulp. Cut reserved cherries in
half; add to soup. Refrigerate
until chilled. Pour chilled soup
into two small bowls placed in
two larger bowls of crushed ice.
Top each serving with dairy
sour cream, if desired.

Cherry Soup for One: Refrigerate one serving no longer
than 2 days.

Manhattan ▲ Clam Chowder

1 slice bacon, cut into ½-in. pieces
1 small red potato, peeled and cut into ½-in. cubes (about ¾ cup)
2 tablespoons chopped onion
2 tablespoons chopped celery
2 tablespoons chopped green pepper
1 teaspoon dried parsley flakes
1 can (12 oz.) vegetable cocktail juice
1 can (6½ oz.) minced clams
¼ teaspoon salt

Serves 2

In 1-qt. casserole combine bacon, potato, onion, celery, green pepper and parsley flakes; cover. Microwave at High 4 to 5 minutes, or until vegetables are tender-crisp. Add juice, undrained clams and salt; cover. Microwave at High 3 to 4 minutes, or until heated, stirring after half the time.

Manhattan Clam Chowder for One: Wrap, label and freeze one serving no longer than 2 weeks. To defrost and heat, microwave at 70% (Medium-High) 6 to 8 minutes, stirring 2 or 3 times.

Cream of Mushroom Soup

1½ cups sliced fresh mushrooms
¼ cup chopped onion
2 tablespoons butter or margarine
2 tablespoons all-purpose flour
2 cups hot water
2 teaspoons instant chicken bouillon granules
½ cup shredded Swiss cheese
⅛ teaspoon white pepper
½ cup half and half
1 teaspoon white wine

Serves 2

In 2-qt. casserole combine mushrooms, onion and butter. Microwave at High 3 to 4 minutes, or until onion is tender, stirring after half the time to coat with butter. Blend in flour. Stir in water and bouillon granules.

Microwave at High 5 to 6 minutes, or until slightly thickened, stirring 2 or 3 times during cooking. Blend in cheese, white pepper, half and half and wine. Microwave at High 2 to 3 minutes, or until heated and cheese melts.

Cream of Mushroom Soup for One: Refrigerate one serving no longer than 2 days. To reheat, microwave at 50% (Medium) 2 to 4 minutes, stirring once or twice during cooking.

Split Pea Soup

1 slice bacon, cut into ½-in. pieces
2 tablespoons chopped onion
3 cups hot water
½ cup dried green split peas
¼ cup sliced carrot, ⅛-in. slices
½ teaspoon salt
¼ teaspoon sugar
2 whole peppercorns
1 small bay leaf

Serves 2

In 2-qt. casserole combine bacon and onion. Cover with paper towel. Microwave at High 2 to 3 minutes, or until bacon is brown. Add remaining ingredients; cover with plastic wrap.

Microwave at High 20 to 35 minutes, or until peas are soft, stirring every 10 minutes. Remove peppercorns and bay leaf before serving.

Split Pea Soup for One: Wrap, label and freeze one serving no longer than 2 weeks. To defrost and heat, microwave at 70% (Medium-High) 6½ to 10 minutes, stirring 2 or 3 times during cooking.

Garden Vegetable Soup ▲

1 can (10¾ oz.) condensed
    chicken broth
1 can (10¾ oz.) hot water
1 teaspoon soy sauce
½ teaspoon sugar
⅛ teaspoon dried thyme leaves
⅛ teaspoon dried basil leaves
⅛ teaspoon onion powder
2 teaspoons cornstarch
¼ lb. fresh broccoli
1 medium carrot, cut into
    2½ × ¼-in. strips
1 cup thinly shredded lettuce,
    page 124

Serves 2

In 2-qt. casserole combine
broth, water, soy sauce, sugar,
thyme, basil and onion powder.
Blend cornstarch into small
amount of broth. Stir back into
broth. Microwave at High 6 to 8
minutes, or until just boiling.

Cut broccoli stems into thin
slices and flowerets into small
pieces. When broth boils add
broccoli and carrot. Microwave
at High 2 to 4½ minutes, or until
vegetables are tender-crisp. Stir
in shredded lettuce.

**Garden Vegetable Soup for
One:** Refrigerate one serving no
longer than 2 days. To reheat,
microwave at High 2 to 4 minutes.

Corn Chowder

1 medium red potato, peeled
    and cut into ½-in. cubes
2 slices bacon, cut into ½-in.
    pieces
¼ cup chopped onion
2 tablespoons all-purpose flour
1 can (13 oz.) evaporated milk
    or 1½ cups half and half
1 can (8½ oz.) cream-style
    corn
¾ teaspoon salt
¼ teaspoon pepper

Serves 2 to 4

Place potato, bacon and onion
in 2-qt. casserole; cover.
Microwave at High 3½ to 5½
minutes, or until potatoes are
fork tender. Stir in flour. Mix in
remaining ingredients. Microwave, uncovered, at High 5 to 8
minutes, or until heated and
slightly thickened, stirring every
2 minutes during cooking.

Corn Chowder for One:
Refrigerate one serving no
longer than 2 days. To reheat,
microwave at 50% (Medium)
5½ to 6½ minutes, stirring once
or twice.

Vichyssoise

1 medium baking potato,
    about 7 oz.
2 tablespoons butter or
    margarine
¼ teaspoon salt
⅛ teaspoon onion powder
    Dash pepper
¾ cup half and half

Serves 1

Scrub potato. Pierce 2 or 3
times with a fork. Place in oven
on paper towel. Microwave at
High 3 to 5 minutes, or until fork
tender, turning over after half
the time. Wrap in foil or place
under inverted bowl. Let stand
5 minutes.

Remove peel from potato.
Quarter and place in deep
bowl. Add butter, salt, onion
powder and pepper. Beat at
medium speed of electric mixer
until smooth, gradually adding
half and half. Pour into serving
bowl. Chill. Sprinkle with
chopped chives, if desired.

Vichyssoise for Two: Double
all ingredients. Prepare as
directed except microwave
potatoes 5 to 7½ minutes.

Fresh Tomato Soup

½ cup vegetable cocktail juice
2 medium tomatoes, cut into
   2-in. cubes
¼ cup chopped onion
¼ cup chopped celery
1 tablespoon butter or
   margarine
1 teaspoon sugar
⅛ teaspoon pepper
3 tablespoons all-purpose flour
2 cups hot water, divided
2 teaspoons instant chicken
   bouillon granules

Serves 2

In 2-qt. casserole combine juice, tomatoes, onion, celery, butter, sugar and pepper. In small bowl mix flour and ¼ cup hot water until smooth. Stir remaining 1¾ cups hot water and bouillon granules in 2-cup measure until dissolved. Pour broth into casserole. Blend in flour mixture; cover.

Microwave at High 10 to 15 minutes, or until tomatoes are tender and mixture is slightly thickened, stirring every 5 minutes. Press through wire strainer. Garnish with parsley or watercress, if desired.

Fresh Tomato Soup for One:
Refrigerate one serving no longer than 2 days. To reheat, microwave at High 3 to 5 minutes, stirring after half the cooking time.

Variation:
Cream of Tomato Soup: Blend ¼ cup whipping cream into prepared soup before serving.

Cream of Tomato Soup for One: Refrigerate one serving no longer than 2 days. To reheat, microwave at 50% (Medium) 5½ to 6½ minutes, stirring after half the cooking time.

Sandwiches

Hot sandwiches make a satisfying lunch or supper. If you're looking for new ideas, this section provides variety as well as basic directions for microwaving one or two sausages or hamburgers. When you microwave bread and filling together, be sure to place the sandwich on a paper towel, which will absorb the moisture from steam trapped between the sandwich and the oven floor.

◄ Tostadas

1 can (8 oz.) kidney beans
3 tablespoons chopped onion, divided
1 tablespoon water
¼ teaspoon ground cumin, divided
¼ teaspoon salt, divided
Dash pepper
¼ lb. ground beef
½ teaspoon chili powder
Dash garlic powder

Dash cayenne pepper
2 tostada shells

Toppings:
½ cup shredded Monterey Jack or Cheddar cheese
½ cup shredded lettuce
¼ cup chopped green pepper
1 medium tomato, chopped
2 tablespoons chopped black olives
Dairy sour cream

Serves 2

In small bowl, mix beans, 1 tablespoon onion, the water, ⅛ teaspoon cumin, ⅛ teaspoon salt and the pepper; cover. Microwave at High 6 to 8 minutes, or until beans mash easily, stirring twice during cooking. Remove cover. Microwave at High 1 to 2 minutes, or until liquid is absorbed.

In small bowl mix ground beef, 2 tablespoons onion, the chili powder, ⅛ teaspoon cumin, ⅛ teaspoon salt, the garlic powder and cayenne. Microwave at High 1 to 3 minutes, or until meat is no longer pink, stirring to break apart 2 or 3 times. Drain.

Place tostada shells on paper towel. Microwave at High 30 to 45 seconds, or until hot to the touch. Spread half of the bean mixture on each shell. Top each with half of the meat mixture. Sprinkle with several or all of the suggested toppings.

Italian Meatball Sandwiches

¼ lb. ground beef
¼ lb. bulk Italian sausage
¼ teaspoon pepper, divided
1 can (8 oz.) tomato sauce
½ teaspoon sugar
¼ teaspoon Italian seasoning
⅛ teaspoon garlic powder
2 hot dog buns

Serves 2

Mix ground beef, sausage and ⅛ teaspoon pepper. Shape into six meatballs. Place in 2-qt. casserole; cover with wax paper. Microwave at High 2 to 3 minutes, or until no longer pink, stirring once or twice. Drain.

Stir in tomato sauce, sugar, Italian seasoning, garlic powder and ⅛ teaspoon pepper. Cover with wax paper. Reduce power to 50% (Medium). Microwave 3 to 5 minutes, or until flavors blend. Spoon into hot dog buns.

Italian Meatball Sandwich for One: Refrigerate half of the filling no longer than 2 days. To reheat, microwave at High 1 to 2½ minutes.

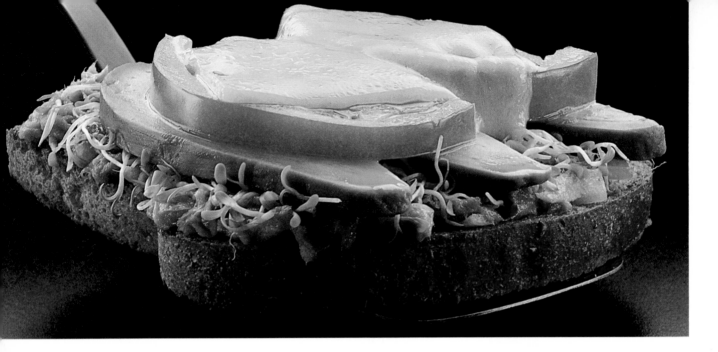

Vegetable-Tuna ▲ Open-Face Sandwiches

2 slices bacon
1 can (3¼ oz.) tuna, drained
2 tablespoons mayonnaise or
　salad dressing
1 tablespoon chopped onion
2 slices whole wheat bread,
　toasted
4 to 6 thin slices avocado
¼ cup alfalfa sprouts
2 slices tomato
2 slices Colby cheese

Serves 2

Place bacon on paper towel-lined plate. Microwave at High 1½ to 2 minutes, or until brown. Crumble. In small bowl mix bacon, tuna, mayonnaise and onion. Spread half evenly on each toast slice. Top with two or three slices avocado, the sprouts, one slice tomato and cheese. Place on paper towel-lined plate. Reduce power to 50% (Medium). Microwave 1½ to 3½ minutes, or until heated and cheese melts.

Vegetable-Tuna Open-Face Sandwich for One: Refrigerate half of the tuna mixture no longer than 1 day. Assemble sandwich, using half the topping amounts. To reheat, microwave at 50% (Medium) 1 to 2 minutes, or until cheese melts.

Crab Meat Croissants

1 tablespoon butter or
　margarine
1 tablespoon chopped green
　onion
1 tablespoon plus 1½ tea-
　spoons all-purpose flour
¼ teaspoon salt
⅛ teaspoon pepper
1 cup half and half
1 teaspoon white wine
1 can (6½ oz.) crab meat,
　rinsed, drained and
　cartilage removed
2 large croissants or 4
　crescent rolls

Serves 2

Place butter and onion in 2-cup measure. Microwave at High 30 to 45 seconds, or until butter melts and onion is tender, stirring after half the time. Stir in flour, salt and pepper. Blend in half and half. Microwave at High 3 to 4 minutes, or until thickened, stirring every minute. Stir in wine and crab meat. Slice croissants in half lengthwise. Spread half of filling on bottom of each. Replace top of croissant.

Crab Meat Croissant for One: Refrigerate half of the filling no longer than 2 days. To reheat, microwave at 50% (Medium) 1½ to 3 minutes, stirring twice. Assemble as directed.

Florentine Croissants

½ lb. fresh spinach, shredded
1 tablespoon butter or
　margarine
1 tablespoon plus 1½ tea-
　spoons all-purpose flour
¼ teaspoon salt
⅛ teaspoon pepper
1 cup half and half
1 teaspoon white wine
2 large croissants or 4
　crescent rolls
¼ lb. thinly sliced ham, cut into
　thin strips

Serves 2

Place spinach in 1½-qt. casserole; cover. Microwave at High 2½ to 3½ minutes, or until tender, stirring once. Drain well. Melt butter in 2-cup measure at High 30 to 45 seconds. Stir in flour, salt and pepper. Blend in half and half. Microwave at High 3 to 4 minutes, or until thickened, stirring with a wire whip after every minute. Stir in wine. Slice croissants in half length-wise. Spread half of spinach on bottom of each. Top each with half the ham, one-fourth the sauce and top of croissant. Add remaining sauce.

Florentine Croissant for One: Refrigerate half of the filling no longer than 2 days. Reheat as directed for Crab Meat Croissant for One.

Hot Deli Melt ▲

1 loaf (8 oz.) French bread,
   cut in half lengthwise
2 tablespoons Poppy Seed
   Dressing, right, or
   mayonnaise
¼ lb. thinly sliced cooked beef,
   turkey or ham

½ cup alfalfa sprouts
1 medium tomato, thinly sliced
½ cup sliced mushrooms
6 to 8 thin slices onion
6 to 8 thin slices green pepper
4 slices (¾ oz. each) Cheddar,
   Colby or Swiss cheese

Serves 2

Spread bread with Poppy Seed Dressing. Layer meat, sprouts,
tomato, mushrooms, onion, green pepper and cheese. Replace
top. Place sandwich on paper towel-lined plate. Microwave at 50%
(Medium) 4 to 6½ minutes, or until cheese melts. Cut in half.

Hot Deli Melt for One: Refrigerate one serving no longer than 2
days. To reheat, wrap in paper towel. Microwave at 70%
(Medium-High) 45 to 60 seconds.

Poppy Seed Dressing

¼ cup mayonnaise or salad
   dressing
¼ teaspoon prepared mustard
⅛ teaspoon poppy seed
   Dash garlic powder

Makes ¼ cup

In a small bowl mix all
ingredients. Use for Hot Deli
Melt or other sandwiches.

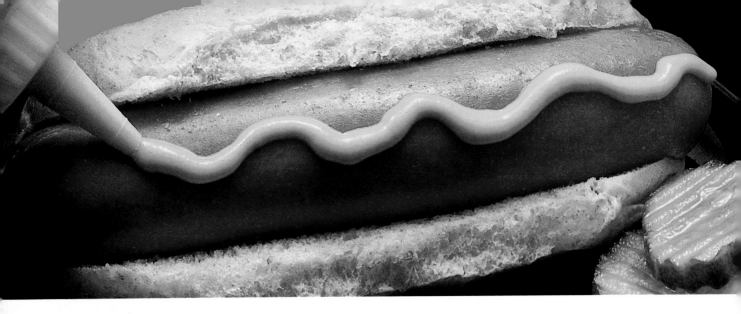

Sausage & Hot Dog Chart

Item	Amount	Microwave Time at High	Procedure
Bratwurst, Polish Sausage (fully cooked)	1 2	¾ - 1¼ min. 1¼ - 1¾ min.	Place sausage in bun. Wrap in paper towel. Microwave until heated, rearranging after half the time.
Hot Dog (fully cooked, 10 to 12/lb.)	1 2	½ - ¾ min. ¾ - 1¼ min.	Microwave as directed, above.

How to Microwave Hamburger Patties

Roasting Rack. Place patties on roasting rack. Brush with equal parts bouquet sauce and water, if desired. Cover with wax paper. Microwave first side. Turn over. Brush with sauce mixture. Cover. Microwave second side. Let stand 1 to 2 minutes.

Browning Dish. Preheat dish according to manufacturers' directions. Place patties in dish. Microwave first side. Turn over. Microwave second side.

Hamburger Patty Chart

Utensil	Number of Patties	Medium Rare		Medium Well	
		1st side	2nd side	1st side	2nd side
Browning Dish	1 2	¾ min. 1 min.	¾ - 1½ min. ¾ - 1½ min.	1½ min. 2 min.	1 - 1½ min. 1 - 2 min.
Roasting Rack	1 2	1 min. 1½ min.	½ - 1½ min. ¾ - 1 min.	1½ min. 2 min.	1 - 1½ min. 1½ - 2½ min.

Lamb Pocket Sandwiches ▶

½ lb. ground lamb
1 slice bacon, cut into ½-in.
   pieces
¼ cup chopped green onion
1 small clove garlic, minced
¼ teaspoon dried mint leaves
¼ teaspoon salt
⅛ teaspoon pepper
1 medium tomato, chopped
¼ cup chopped cucumber
¼ cup snipped fresh parsley
2 pita loaves, 5-in. diameter

Serves 2

Crumble lamb into 1½-qt. casserole. Add bacon, green onion, garlic, mint, salt and pepper. Cover with paper towel. Microwave at High 2 to 3 minutes, or until meat is no longer pink, stirring to break apart after half the time. Drain. Stir in tomato, cucumber and parsley. Slice each loaf in half to form pockets. Spoon filling into pockets.

Canadian Bagel

1 tablespoon (½ oz.) cream
   cheese
1 teaspoon chopped green
   onion
1 plain bagel, split and toasted
1 slice Canadian bacon
2 tablespoons shredded
   Cheddar cheese

Serves 1

Place cream cheese in small bowl. Microwave at High 10 to 20 seconds, or until softened. Stir in green onion. Spread on toasted bagel. Top with bacon and cheese. Replace bagel top. Wrap in paper towel. Reduce power to 50% (Medium). Microwave 30 to 45 seconds, or until warm to the touch.

Canadian Bagels for Two:
Double all ingredients. Prepare as directed except microwave cream cheese at High 15 to 20 seconds. Reduce power to 50% (Medium). Microwave bagels 45 seconds to 1¼ minutes.

General Meat Tips

For small households, it pays to shop in a market which provides the services of a butcher. When you can't find pre-packaged meat in the amount you need, ask for what you want. If you are storing meat for several days, remove from store or butcher's package and wrap loosely in plastic wrap before refrigerating it.

To take advantage of a sale price on larger cuts, divide fresh meat into small roasts, strips and chunks, as directed in this section. Freeze in single portions as directed on page 8. Bacon and ham should not be frozen, but keep well in the refrigerator.

When defrosting small amounts of meat, allow ample standing time. If you try to defrost meat completely with microwave energy, the outer portions can begin to cook before the center is thawed.

Meat Storage Chart

Type	Single Serving Size	Maximum Refrigerator Time	Maximum Freezer Time
Bacon	2 strips	1 week	Do not freeze
Chops	¼ to ⅓ lb.	3 to 5 days	4 months
Flat Roasts, Large Steaks	¼ to ⅓ lb.	3 to 5 days	6 months
Ground	¼ lb.	1 to 2 days	3 months
Ham, fresh	¼ to ⅓ lb.	1 week	Do not freeze
canned	¼ to ⅓ lb.	Opened: 1 week Unopened: 6 months	Do not freeze
Liver	¼ lb.	1 to 2 days	4 months
Ribs	¾ lb.	3 to 5 days	3 months
Sausage	¼ lb.	2 to 3 days	3 months
Stew Meat	⅓ lb.	1 to 2 days	6 months
Strips	¼ lb.	1 to 2 days	6 months

How to Defrost Meat

Remove wrapping from meat. Place meat in baking dish or elevate on roasting rack.

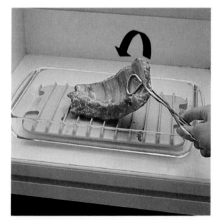

Microwave and turn over, rotate or break apart as directed in chart, opposite. Meat will still be partially frozen, but will defrost during standing time.

Let stand as directed in chart, or until wooden skewer can be inserted easily to center.

Meat Defrosting Chart

Type	Defrost Time at 50% (Medium)	Procedure
Beef		
Ground	3 - 5 min./lb.	Follow photo directions, breaking apart after half the time. Let stand 3 to 5 minutes.
Flat Roasts, Large Steaks	3½ - 4½ min./lb.	Follow photo directions, rotating and turning over 3 or 4 times. Shield as needed. Let stand 5 minutes.
Liver	5 - 7 min./lb.	Follow photo directions, turning over and separating pieces 3 times during defrosting. Let stand 5 minutes.
Stew Meat	3 - 5½ min./lb.	Follow photo directions, breaking apart and turning over after half the time. Let stand 5 to 10 minutes.
Pork		
Ground	3 - 5 min./lb.	Follow photo directions, breaking apart after half the time. Let stand 3 to 5 minutes.
Chops	3½ - 6 min./lb.	Follow photo directions, turning over after half the time. Let stand 10 minutes.
Roast	6¼ - 9 min./lb.	Follow photo directions, rotating and turning over 3 or 4 times. Shield as needed. Let stand 20 to 30 minutes.
Ribs	3 - 6 min./lb.	Follow photo directions, breaking apart and rearranging after half the time. Let stand 10 to 15 minutes.
Bulk Sausage	3 min./lb.	Follow photo directions, rearranging and turning over after half the time. Let stand 20 to 30 minutes.
Lamb		
Ground	3 - 5 min./lb.	Follow photo directions, breaking apart after half the time. Let stand 3 to 5 minutes.
Chops	4 - 6½ min./lb.	Follow photo directions, turning over after half the time. Let stand 10 minutes.
Roast	5 - 8 min./lb.	Follow photo directions, rotating and turning over 3 or 4 times. Shield as needed. Let stand 15 to 20 minutes.
Stew Meat	4½ - 6½ min./lb.	Follow photo directions, breaking apart and turning over after half the time. Let stand 5 to 10 minutes.
Veal		
Ground	3 - 5 min./lb.	Follow photo directions, breaking apart after half the time. Let stand 3 to 5 minutes.
Chops	4 - 6 min./lb.	Follow photo directions, turning over after half the time. Let stand 10 minutes.
Round Steak	3 - 4 min./lb.	Follow photo directions, turning over after half the time. Let stand 5 minutes.
Stew Meat	3 - 5½ min./lb.	Follow photo directions, breaking apart and turning over after half the time. Let stand 5 to 10 minutes.

Making the Most of Round Steak

You can purchase top or bottom round steak, but it is more economical to buy a whole 1-in. thick steak, weighing 2¾ to 3 pounds, and cut it up.

To make cutting easier, partially freeze the steak for 1 to 1½ hours. After cutting, wrap, label and freeze the pieces. The

large top round section divides neatly into rouladen or strips. Use the smaller bottom round piece for Swiss steak or stew.

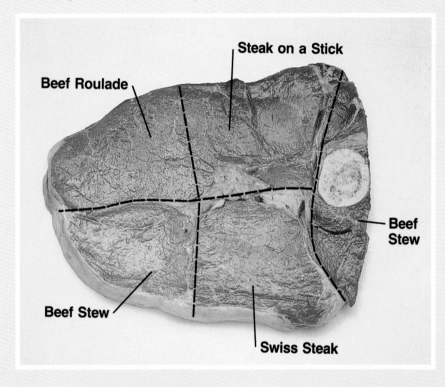

Beef Roulade

Steak on a Stick

Beef Stew

Beef Stew

Swiss Steak

Swiss Steak: Cut ½-lb. bottom round steak horizontally into two ½-in. thick slices. Wrap individually, label and freeze no longer than 6 months. To defrost, microwave one at 50% (Medium) 2½ to 4 minutes, turning over every minute. If meat begins to cook around edges, let stand to complete defrosting.

Steak on a Stick: Cut ¾-lb. top round steak across grain in ⅛-in. wide strips. Wrap, label and freeze no longer than 6 months. To defrost, microwave at 50% (Medium) 3 to 4 minutes, breaking apart, removing any defrosted portions and turning over after half the time.

Beef Stew: Cut ¾-lb. beef bottom round steak into ½-in. cubes. Wrap, label and freeze no longer than 6 months. To defrost, microwave at 50% (Medium) 3 to 4 minutes, breaking apart, removing any defrosted portions and turning over after half the time.

Beef Roulade: Cut ½-lb. top round steak horizontally into two ½-in. thick slices. Each slice makes one roulade. Wrap individually, label and freeze no longer than 6 months. To defrost, microwave one at 50% (Medium) 2½ to 4 minutes, turning over every minute. If meat begins to cook around edges, let stand to complete defrosting. Pound as directed in recipe, page 38.

Swiss Steak ▲

½ lb. beef boneless bottom
  round steak, cut into
  2 pieces, page 36
1 tablespoon all-purpose flour
¼ teaspoon salt
⅛ teaspoon pepper
1 can (8 oz.) stewed tomatoes
¼ cup chopped onion
1 tablespoon French dressing
⅛ teaspoon dried rosemary
  leaves
2 green pepper rings, optional

Serves 2

Pound meat to ¼-in. thickness
with edge of saucer or meat
mallet. In paper or plastic bag
mix flour, salt and pepper.
Shake meat in bag until coated.
Place meat in 2-qt. square
casserole. Mix tomatoes, onion,
dressing and rosemary; pour
over meat. Place green pepper
rings on top of meat; cover.
Microwave at 50% (Medium) 25
minutes. Turn meat over. Spoon
sauce over meat. Microwave,
covered, at 50% (Medium) 15 to
25 minutes, or until tender. Let
stand, covered, 10 minutes.

Swiss Steak for One: Refrigerate one serving no longer than
2 days. To reheat, microwave at
50% (Medium) 5 to 7 minutes,
stirring sauce and turning meat
after half the time.

Steak on a Stick

1 small orange
¾ lb. beef boneless top round
  steak, cut into ⅛-in.
  strips, page 36
4 wooden skewers, 10-in. long
1 tablespoon packed brown
  sugar
⅛ teaspoon salt
⅛ teaspoon pepper
¼ cup catsup
1 tablespoon prepared
  mustard
1 tablespoon chopped onion
1 teaspoon vinegar
3 or 4 drops red pepper sauce

Serves 2

Cut orange in half crosswise.
Cut one half into four wedges.
Squeeze 1 tablespoon juice
from remaining half. Set aside.
Weave four or five steak strips
on each skewer in "S" shape.
Place one orange wedge on
each skewer. In 2-cup measure
mix remaining ingredients with
reserved 1 tablespoon orange
juice. Microwave at High 1
minute. Stir. Place kabobs on
roasting rack. Baste all sides
with sauce. Cover with plastic
wrap; refrigerate 2 hours.
Remove plastic wrap. Reduce
power to 50% (Medium).
Microwave 10 to 14 minutes, or
until desired doneness, rotating
and rearranging skewers 3 or 4
times during cooking.

Beef Stew

¾ lb. beef boneless bottom
  round steak, cut into ½-in.
  cubes, page 36
3 tablespoons cornstarch
½ teaspoon salt
⅛ teaspoon pepper
2 cups hot water
1 medium carrot, thinly sliced
1 stalk celery, thinly sliced
1 medium potato, peeled and
  cut into ½-in. cubes
1 small onion, cut into eighths
½ cup frozen cut green beans
1 tablespoon snipped fresh
  parsley
½ teaspoon bouquet sauce

Serves 2

In 3-qt. casserole toss meat with
cornstarch, salt and pepper
until coated. Stir in remaining
ingredients; cover. Microwave at
High 5 minutes. Stir. Reduce
power to 50% (Medium). Microwave 30 to 45 minutes, or until
meat and vegetables are tender, stirring 3 or 4 times during
cooking. Remove cover during
last 5 minutes of cooking time.
Let stand, covered, 10 minutes.

Beef Stew for One: Wrap, label
and freeze one serving no
longer than 2 weeks. To defrost
and heat, microwave at 70%
(Medium-High) 9 to 11 minutes,
stirring 2 or 3 times.

Beef Roulade

¼ lb. beef boneless top round
   steak, ½-in. thick, page 36
Unseasoned meat tenderizer
¼ cup unseasoned stuffing mix
1 tablespoon uncooked
   instant rice
¼ teaspoon dried parsley
   flakes
Dash ground sage
1½ teaspoons diced celery
½ teaspoon olive oil
3 tablespoons water
½ teaspoon bouquet sauce

Gravy:

1½ teaspoons butter or
   margarine
1½ teaspoons all-purpose flour
¼ cup hot water
½ teaspoon red wine
⅛ teaspoon instant beef
   bouillon granules
⅛ teaspoon bouquet sauce
Dash salt
Dash pepper

Serves 1

Beef Rouladen for Two:
Double all ingredients. Prepare as directed except microwave celery and olive oil at High 2 to 3 minutes. Add water; microwave at High 1 to 2 minutes. Reduce power to 50% (Medium). Microwave rouladen 9 to 12 minutes, turning after 5 minutes. Increase power to High. Microwave gravy 1½ to 2½ minutes.

How to Microwave Beef Roulade

Sprinkle surface of meat with tenderizer. Pound to ¼-in. thickness with meat mallet or edge of saucer held at right angle to meat. In small bowl mix stuffing mix, rice, parsley and sage. Set aside.

Place celery and olive oil in 2-cup measure. Cover with plastic wrap. Microwave at High 1 to 2 minutes, or until celery is tender, stirring after half the time. Add water; cover.

Microwave at High 1½ to 2 minutes, or until boiling. Pour over bread stuffing mixture, tossing to moisten. Cover with plastic wrap. Let stand 5 minutes to absorb moisture.

Spread stuffing mixture to within ¼ inch from edge of meat. Roll up jelly-roll style. Secure with wooden picks. Brush with bouquet sauce. Place on roasting rack or trivet. Reduce power to 50% (Medium).

Microwave 6 to 8 minutes, or until heated and meat is desired doneness, turning over after half the time. Let stand while preparing gravy. Increase power to High.

Melt butter in 2-cup measure at High 30 to 45 seconds. Blend in flour. Stir in remaining gravy ingredients until smooth. Microwave at High 30 to 60 seconds, or until thickened, stirring once. Serve over roulade.

Making the Most of Sirloin Steak

Sirloin is a tender cut and needs less cooking time than round steak. The cost per pound is usually lower than other tender steaks. Sirloin is identified by the shape of the bone. Flat bone and round bone sirloin are widely available, with pin bone less frequently found. The flat bone in a 2-lb. steak weighs about half a pound, leaving about 1½ pounds of meat to cut into six servings. The meat is easy to cube. To make strips easier to cut, partially freeze the steak for 1 to 1½ hours. After cutting, wrap, label and freeze.

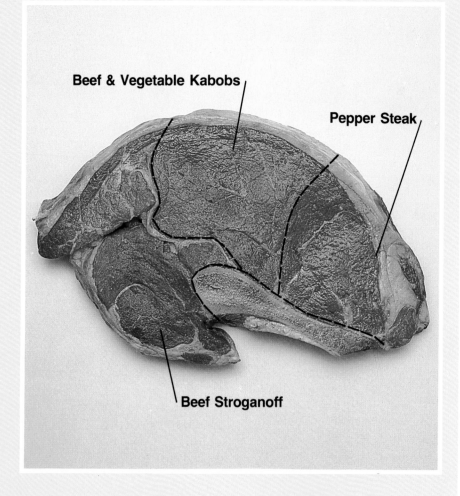

Beef & Vegetable Kabobs

Pepper Steak

Beef Stroganoff

Pepper Steak: Cut ½-lb. sirloin steak into ¼-in. strips. Wrap, label and freeze no longer than 6 months. To defrost, microwave at 50% (Medium) 2½ to 3 minutes, breaking apart, removing any defrosted portions and turning over after half the time.

Beef & Vegetable Kabob: Cut ½-lb. sirloin steak into 1-in. cubes. Wrap, label and freeze in ¼-lb. packages no longer than 6 months. To defrost, microwave ¼-lb. at 50% (Medium) 1 to 2 minutes, and ½-lb. for 2½ to 3 minutes, breaking apart, removing any defrosted portions and turning over after half the time.

Beef Stroganoff: Cut ½-lb. sirloin steak into ½-in. cubes. Wrap, label and freeze no longer than 6 months. To defrost, microwave at 50% (Medium) 2½ to 3 minutes, breaking apart, removing any defrosted portions and turning over after half the time.

Pepper Steak

- 1 tablespoon packed brown sugar
- ⅛ teaspoon garlic powder
- 3 tablespoons water
- 2 tablespoons soy sauce
- 1 tablespoon lemon juice
- ½ lb. beef boneless sirloin steak, cut into ¼-in. strips, opposite
- 2 green onions, sliced diagonally
- 1 medium carrot, cut into matchstick pieces
- 1 medium green pepper, cut into ¼-in. strips
- ½ red pepper, cut into ¼-in. strips
- 1½ teaspoons cornstarch

Serves 2

In small bowl mix brown sugar, garlic powder, water, soy sauce and lemon juice. Stir in meat until coated; cover. Marinate at room temperature 30 minutes or in refrigerator 1 hour.

Combine green onions, carrot, green and red pepper in 2-qt. casserole. Drain marinade from meat; add to vegetables. Cover. Microwave at High 4 minutes, stirring after half the cooking time. Add meat.

Microwave, uncovered, at High 4 to 5½ minutes, or until desired doneness, stirring 2 or 3 times. Drain liquid into 2-cup measure. Gradually stir in cornstarch until smooth. Microwave at High 1 to 2 minutes, or until thickened, stirring after the first minute, then every 30 seconds. Pour over beef and vegetables. Serve over rice, page 133, if desired.

Pepper Steak for One: Wrap, label and freeze one serving no longer than 2 weeks. To defrost and heat, microwave at 70% (Medium-High) 5 to 8 minutes, stirring after half the time to break apart.

◀ Beef & Vegetable Kabob

1 tablespoon butter or
    margarine
¼ teaspoon dried parsley flakes
1 small clove garlic, minced
¼ teaspoon grated Parmesan
    cheese
1 wooden skewer, 10-in. long
¼ lb. beef boneless sirloin
    steak, cut into 1-in. cubes,
    page 40
2 cherry tomatoes
1 small onion, cut in half
2 pieces zucchini, ½-in. thick

Serves 1

In 1-cup measure combine butter, parsley flakes and garlic. Microwave at High 30 seconds, or until butter melts. Stir in cheese. Set aside.

Alternate beef cubes with vegetables on skewer, leaving space between. Place on roasting rack. Brush with half the butter mixture. Reduce power to 50% (Medium). Microwave 4 to 8 minutes, rotating and turning over after 3 minutes and brushing with remaining butter. Check for doneness by cutting into meat after half the cooking time. Meat may appear pink outside.

Beef & Vegetable Kabobs for Two: Double all ingredients. Prepare as directed except microwave at 50% (Medium) 6 to 9 minutes, rotating and turning twice during cooking.

Beef Stroganoff ▲

½ lb. beef boneless sirloin
    steak, cut into ½-in.
    cubes, page 40
¼ cup chopped onion
1 teaspoon instant beef
    bouillon granules
1 cup hot water
1½ tablespoons cornstarch
½ teaspoon dried basil leaves
¼ teaspoon paprika
⅛ teaspoon pepper
½ cup plain yogurt or dairy
    sour cream
1 can (2½ oz.) sliced
    mushrooms, drained

Serves 2

Place meat and onion in 1½-qt. casserole; cover. Microwave at 50% (Medium) 8 to 10 minutes, or until meat is tender, stirring 3 times. Remove meat and onion. Dissolve bouillon in water; stir into casserole with cornstarch, basil, paprika and pepper. Increase power to High. Microwave 3 to 4 minutes, or until thickened, stirring 3 times. Add meat, onion, yogurt and mushrooms; cover. Reduce power to 50% (Medium). Microwave 5 to 7 minutes, or until heated. Let stand, covered, 5 minutes. Serve over egg noodles, page 131, if desired.

Beef Stroganoff for One: Refrigerate one serving no longer than 2 days. To reheat, microwave, covered, at 70% (Medium-High) 5 to 6½ minutes, stirring after half the time.

Making the Most of Pot Roast

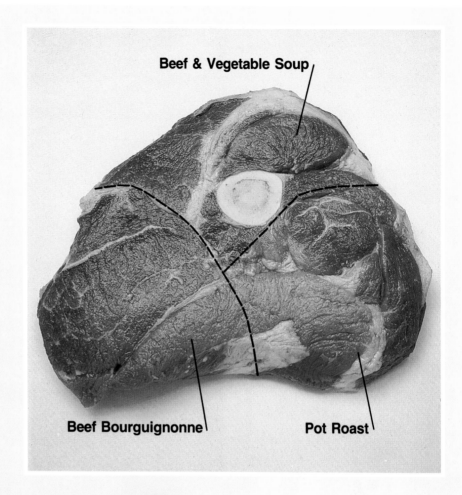

Beef & Vegetable Soup

Beef Bourguignonne

Pot Roast

Economical pot roast is a flavorful cut of beef which requires moisture and longer cooking to tenderize. A 2¾- to 3-lb. arm bone pot roast divides to make three different recipes.

First, cut out the large, solid piece to make a 1-lb. boneless pot roast for two. Trim away the fat and cut remaining meat into ½-in. cubes to make soup and Beef Bourguignonne. Divide the cubes into two packages and include the bone with the soup meat. The marrow and gelatin from the bone will add body to your soup.

Beef & Vegetable Soup: Use ¾-lb. piece of pot roast with bone. Cut meat into ½-in. cubes. Wrap, label and freeze no longer than 6 months. To defrost, microwave at 50% (Medium) 5 to 7 minutes, breaking apart, removing any defrosted portions and turning over after half the time. If meat begins to cook around edges, let stand to complete defrosting.

Pot Roast: Use 1-lb. piece of boneless pot roast. Wrap, label and freeze no longer than 6 months. To defrost, microwave at 50% (Medium) 9 to 11 minutes, turning over after half the time. If meat begins to cook around edges, let stand to complete defrosting.

Beef Bourguignonne: Cut ½-lb. pot roast into ½-in. cubes. Wrap, label and freeze no longer than 6 months. To defrost, microwave at 50% (Medium) 3 to 6 minutes, breaking apart, removing any defrosted portions and turning over after half the time.

◄ Pot Roast

1 lb. beef boneless arm pot
  roast, page 43
¾ cup beer, water or tomato
  juice, divided
¼ teaspoon salt
⅛ teaspoon pepper
2 new potatoes, peeled and
  quartered
1 medium carrot, cut
  lengthwise in half, then
  into 2-in. pieces
1 celery stalk, cut
  lengthwise in half, then
  into 3-in. pieces
1 small onion, quartered

Serves 2

Pierce both sides of meat
thoroughly with fork. Place in
2-qt. square casserole. Mix half
of the beer, the salt and the
pepper. Pour over meat; cover.
Microwave at 50% (Medium) 40
minutes, turning over 2 or 3
times during cooking. Arrange
vegetables around sides of
meat. Pour remaining beer over
meat and vegetables; cover.
Microwave at 50% (Medium) 25
to 35 minutes, or until meat is
fork tender. Let stand, covered,
5 minutes.

Pot Roast for One: Refrigerate
one serving no longer than 2
days. To reheat, microwave at
50% (Medium) 6 to 7 minutes,
turning over after half the time.

Beef Bourguignonne ▲

1 slice bacon, cut up
½ lb. beef boneless arm pot
  roast, cut into ½-in.
  cubes, page 43
¼ cup all-purpose flour
1 can (10¾ oz.) condensed
  beef broth
⅓ cup red cooking wine
¼ cup chopped onion
½ teaspoon dried parsley flakes
⅛ teaspoon garlic powder
⅛ teaspoon pepper
1 small bay leaf
  Dash dried thyme leaves
1 can (2½ oz.) sliced
  mushrooms, drained
⅓ cup slivered almonds

Serves 2

Place bacon pieces in 3-qt.
casserole. Microwave at High
45 to 60 seconds, or until
brown. Add meat and flour,
tossing to coat. Stir in remaining
ingredients except mushrooms
and almonds; cover. Microwave
at High 5 minutes. Stir. Reduce
power to 50% (Medium).
Microwave, covered, 35 to 50
minutes, or until meat is tender.
Stir in mushrooms. Microwave,
uncovered, at 50% (Medium) 5
minutes, or until thickened. Let
stand, covered, 10 minutes. Add
almonds before serving. Serve
over rice, page 133, if desired.

Beef Bourguignonne for One:
Refrigerate one serving no
longer than 2 days. To reheat,
microwave at 70% (Medium-
High) 3 to 4 minutes, stirring
after half the time.

Beef & Vegetable Soup

¾ lb. beef arm pot roast with
  bone, cut into ½-in.
  cubes, page 43
3 cups water
⅓ cup thinly sliced carrot
⅓ cup thinly sliced celery
¼ cup chopped onion
2 tablespoons pearl barley
1 tablespoon instant beef
  bouillon granules
¼ teaspoon dried savory,
  basil or marjoram leaves
⅛ teaspoon garlic powder
⅛ teaspoon pepper
1 can (8¾ oz.) whole kernel
  corn, drained
½ cup frozen cut green beans

Makes 3 cups

Combine all ingredients except
corn and beans in 3-qt. casserole. Cover. Microwave at High
10 minutes. Remove marrow
from bone, return marrow to
soup. Discard bone. Reduce
power to 50% (Medium). Microwave, covered, 50 minutes,
stirring 2 or 3 times. Add corn
and green beans. Microwave at
50% (Medium) 10 to 20
minutes, or until meat and
vegetables are tender.

**Beef & Vegetable Soup for
One:** Wrap, label and freeze
one serving no longer than 2
weeks. To defrost and heat,
microwave, covered, at 70%
(Medium-High) 10 to 14
minutes, stirring 2 or 3 times
during cooking to break apart.
Let stand 5 minutes.

Making the Most of Ground Beef

Ground beef is packaged in amounts of 1 pound or more, but you can buy as little as ¼ pound. Simply ask the butcher for what you need. Fresh ground beef should be used within 24 hours. Freeze extra ground beef in ¼- to ½-lb. packages. Store no longer than 3 months.

Recipes that use ground beef:
Chili, below
Meatloaf, opposite
Swedish Meatballs, opposite
Lasagna Rolls, page 48
Beef & Bean Burritos, page 49
Spaghetti Sauce, page 49

How to Defrost Ground Beef

Place unwrapped frozen ground beef in 1-qt. casserole or defrost in freezer wrap at 50% (Medium) as directed in chart, breaking apart after half the time. Let stand 3 to 5 minutes to complete defrosting.

Amount	Microwave Time
¼ lb.	2 minutes
½ lb.	2½ - 3 minutes

How to Microwave Ground Beef

Crumble ground beef into 1-qt. casserole. Microwave at High as directed in chart, or until meat is no longer pink, stirring after half the cooking time to break apart.

Amount	Microwave Time
¼ lb.	1 - 3 minutes
½ lb.	3 - 4 minutes

◄ Chili

½ lb. ground beef
¼ cup chopped onion
2 tablespoons chopped green pepper
1 can (16 oz.) whole tomatoes
1 can (8 oz.) kidney beans, drained

2 tablespoons tomato paste
4 drops red pepper sauce
1½ teaspoons sugar
1 teaspoon chili powder
1 teaspoon salt
⅛ teaspoon pepper

Serves 2

Crumble ground beef in 2-qt. casserole. Add onion and green pepper; cover. Microwave at High 4 to 5 minutes, or until meat is no longer pink and vegetables are tender, stirring to break apart after half the time. Drain. Stir in remaining ingredients. Microwave at High 14 to 18 minutes, or until flavors are blended and of desired consistency, stirring 3 or 4 times during cooking.

Variation:
Chili-Mac: Prepare one serving elbow macaroni as directed, page 131. Stir into hot chili.

Chili for One: Wrap, label and freeze one serving no longer than 2 weeks. To defrost and heat, microwave at 70% (Medium-High) 6½ to 10 minutes, stirring 2 or 3 times during cooking.

Meat Loaf ▲

½ lb. ground beef
1 slice soft white bread,
   crumbled
2 tablespoons milk
1 tablespoon chopped onion
2 tablespoons catsup, divided
1 teaspoon Worcestershire
   sauce
⅛ teaspoon garlic powder
⅛ teaspoon salt
   Dash pepper

Serves 2

Crumble ground beef in medium bowl. Mix in crumbled bread, milk, onion, 1 tablespoon catsup, the Worcestershire sauce, garlic powder, salt and pepper. Shape into small loaf. Place in 6½ × 4-in. loaf dish. Microwave at High 3 minutes, rotating after half the time. Brush with remaining 1 tablespoon catsup. Garnish with green pepper slice, if desired. Microwave at High 1 to 2½ minutes, or until internal temperature reaches 145° to 155°F., rotating ½ turn after half the time and removing drippings as necessary. Let stand, uncovered, 2 minutes.

Swedish Meatballs

Meatballs:

¼ lb. ground beef
1 slice soft white bread,
   crumbled
2 teaspoons milk
¾ teaspoon dried minced onion
⅛ teaspoon salt
   Dash pepper

Sauce:

1 tablespoon all-purpose flour
½ teaspoon instant beef
   bouillon granules
½ teaspoon parsley flakes
⅛ teaspoon ground nutmeg
   Dash salt
   Dash pepper
¼ cup hot water
½ cup milk

Serves 2

In small bowl, mix all meatball ingredients. Shape into eight meatballs. Arrange around edge of 1-qt. square casserole. Microwave at High 1 to 1½ minutes, or until meatballs are no longer pink, turning over after half the time. Drain, reserving 1 tablespoon drippings.

In 4-cup measure mix flour, bouillon granules, parsley, nutmeg, salt and pepper. Stir in water and reserved drippings until smooth. Gradually blend in milk. Microwave at High 3½ to 4½ minutes, or until slightly thickened, stirring after the first minute and then every 30 seconds.

Pour sauce over meatballs. Microwave at High 2 to 3 minutes, or until meatballs are firm and centers are no longer pink, stirring after half the cooking time. Serve meatballs over hot cooked egg noodles, page 131, if desired.

Lasagna Rolls

2 lasagna noodles, page 131
¼ lb. ground beef
1 tablespoon chopped onion
½ cup tomato juice
2 tablespoons tomato paste
1 teaspoon sugar
¼ teaspoon salt
¼ teaspoon dried oregano
    leaves
¼ teaspoon dried basil leaves,
    divided
    Dash pepper
¼ cup cottage cheese
¼ cup shredded mozzarella
    cheese, divided
2 tablespoons grated
    Parmesan cheese
⅛ teaspoon garlic powder

Serves 2

Lasagna Roll for One: Wrap,
label and freeze one roll no
longer than 2 weeks. To defrost
and heat, microwave at 50%
(Medium) 9 to 11 minutes,
rotating after half the time.

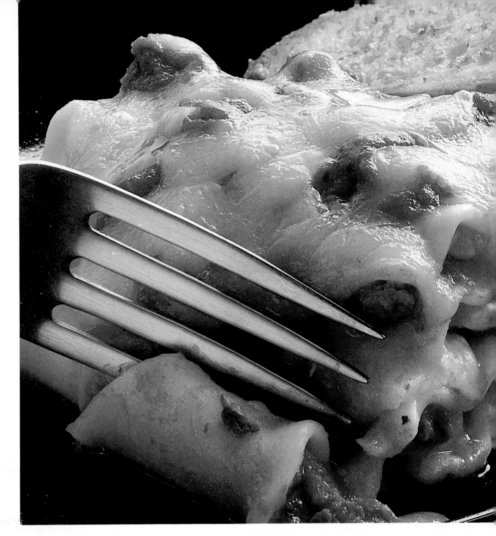

How to Microwave Lasagna Rolls

Prepare lasagna noodles as
directed. Place ground beef
and onion in 1-qt. casserole.
Microwave at High 1 to 3
minutes, or until meat is no
longer pink, stirring to break
apart after half the time. Drain.
Stir in tomato juice, tomato
paste, sugar, salt, oregano, ⅛
teaspoon basil and the pepper.

Microwave meat mixture at
High 4 to 7 minutes, or until
thickened and flavors blend,
stirring twice. Remove ¼ cup
ground beef mixture; set aside.
In small bowl combine cottage
cheese, 2 tablespoons
mozzarella cheese, the
Parmesan cheese, garlic and
remaining ⅛ teaspoon basil.

Spread half of the remaining
ground beef mixture down the
center of each lasagna noodle.
Top with half of the cheese
mixture. Roll up noodles. Place
rolls seam side down in 14-oz.
oval casserole.

48

Top with reserved meat mixture and sprinkle with remaining 2 tablespoons mozzarella cheese; cover. Reduce power to 50% (Medium). Microwave 4 to 5 minutes, or until rolls are heated and cheese melts, rotating dish ½ turn after half the time.

Beef & Bean Burritos ▲

½ lb. ground beef
¼ cup chopped onion
1 can (10½ oz.) bean dip
2 tablespoons taco, salsa or tomato sauce
½ teaspoon ground cumin
½ teaspoon dried oregano leaves
4 flour tortillas, 10-in. diameter
1 cup shredded Cheddar cheese

Makes 4

Crumble ground beef into 1-qt. casserole. Add onion. Cover with paper towel. Microwave at High 3 to 5 minutes, or until meat is no longer pink, stirring after half the time to break apart. Drain. Stir in bean dip, taco sauce, cumin and oregano. Microwave at High 3 to 4 minutes, or until bubbly. Place ½ cup in center of each tortilla. Sprinkle each with ¼ cup cheese. Fold two sides in to center and roll up. Microwave two burritos at a time on plate at High 1 to 2 minutes, or until heated through.

Beef & Bean Burritos for One:
Wrap, label and freeze extra rolled up burritos no longer than 2 weeks. To defrost and heat, microwave one burrito at High 2 to 3 minutes and two burritos 2½ to 4 minutes, rearranging after half the time.

Spaghetti Sauce

½ lb. ground beef
¼ cup chopped onion
1 small clove garlic, minced
1 can (8 oz.) tomato sauce
1 medium tomato, peeled and chopped
1½ teaspoons Worcestershire sauce
1 teaspoon sugar
½ teaspoon salt
¼ teaspoon dried oregano leaves
¼ teaspoon dried basil leaves
⅛ teaspoon pepper
1 medium bay leaf

Makes 2 cups

Place ground beef, onion and garlic in 2-qt. casserole. Microwave at High 3 to 4 minutes, or until meat is no longer pink, stirring to break apart after half the time. Drain. Stir in remaining ingredients; cover. Microwave at High 8 to 10 minutes, or until tomatoes are soft and sauce is thickened, stirring 2 or 3 times during cooking. Serve over spaghetti, page 131, if desired.

Spaghetti Sauce for One:
Wrap, label and freeze half the sauce no longer than 2 weeks. To defrost and heat, micro-wave at 70% (Medium-High) 5 to 9 minutes.

Making the Most of Veal Round Steak

One veal round steak, sliced ¼ inch thick and weighing ¾ to 1 pound, will make three servings of meat, which you may use in several ways. Separate the top and bottom round, discarding bone. Cut the bottom round into ½-in. pieces for one serving of Veal With Noodles & Cheese. Divide the top round into two steaks. Each steak makes one serving of Double Cheese Veal Roll or Tarragon Steak. If cut into strips, each steak makes one serving of Veal Italian.

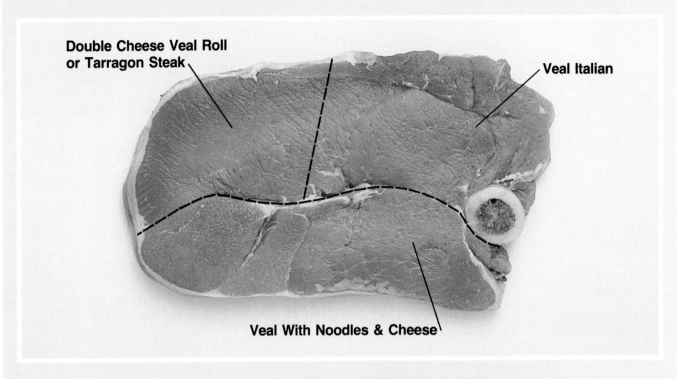

Double Cheese Veal Roll or Tarragon Steak

Veal Italian

Veal With Noodles & Cheese

Double Cheese Veal Roll or Tarragon Steak. Cut ¼-lb. top round steak. Wrap, label and freeze no longer than 6 months. To defrost, microwave at 50% (Medium) 1 to 2 minutes, turning over every minute. If meat begins to cook around edges, let stand to complete defrosting. Pound as directed in recipes.

Veal Italian. Cut ¼-lb. top round steak into ½-in. strips. Wrap, label and freeze no longer than 6 months. To defrost, microwave at 50% (Medium) 1 to 2 minutes, breaking apart, removing any defrosted portions and turning over after half the time.

Veal With Noodles & Cheese. Cut ¼-lb. bottom round steak into ½-in. pieces. Wrap, label and freeze no longer than 6 months. To defrost, microwave at 50% (Medium) 1 to 2 minutes, breaking apart, removing any defrosted portions and turning over after half the time.

Double Cheese Veal Roll

¼ lb. veal boneless top round
   steak, page 50
½ slice (1 oz.) fully cooked ham
 1 teaspoon grated Parmesan
   cheese
⅛ teaspoon pepper
⅛ teaspoon ground ginger,
   divided
 2 teaspoons corn flake crumbs
¼ teaspoon dried parsley
   flakes, divided
 1 teaspoon butter or margarine
 1 teaspoon all-purpose flour
   Dash salt
 2 tablespoons milk
 1 tablespoon grated Monterey
   Jack cheese

Serves 1

Pound both sides of veal steak
with edge of saucer or meat
mallet. Place ham slice on veal
steak. Sprinkle with Parmesan
cheese, pepper and dash
ginger. Roll up tightly. Secure
with wooden pick. In small dish
mix corn flake crumbs and ⅛
teaspoon parsley flakes. Roll
meat in crumb mixture. Place
coated meat in 14-oz. oval
individual casserole. Cover with
wax paper. Microwave at 50%
(Medium) 2½ to 3 minutes, or
until meat is no longer pink,
turning roll over twice. Drain.
Set aside, covered.

Increase power to High.
Microwave butter in 2-cup
measure 15 to 20 seconds, or
until melted. Stir in flour, salt,
remaining dash of ginger and ⅛
teaspoon parsley flakes. Blend
in milk. Microwave at High 15 to
30 seconds, or until thickened,
stirring once. Stir in cheese until
melted. Pour sauce over roll.

**Double Cheese Veal Rolls for
Two:** Double all ingredients.
Prepare as directed except
microwave meat at 50%
(Medium) 3½ to 4 minutes.
Increase power to High.
Microwave butter 30 to 45
seconds; sauce at High 45 to
60 seconds.

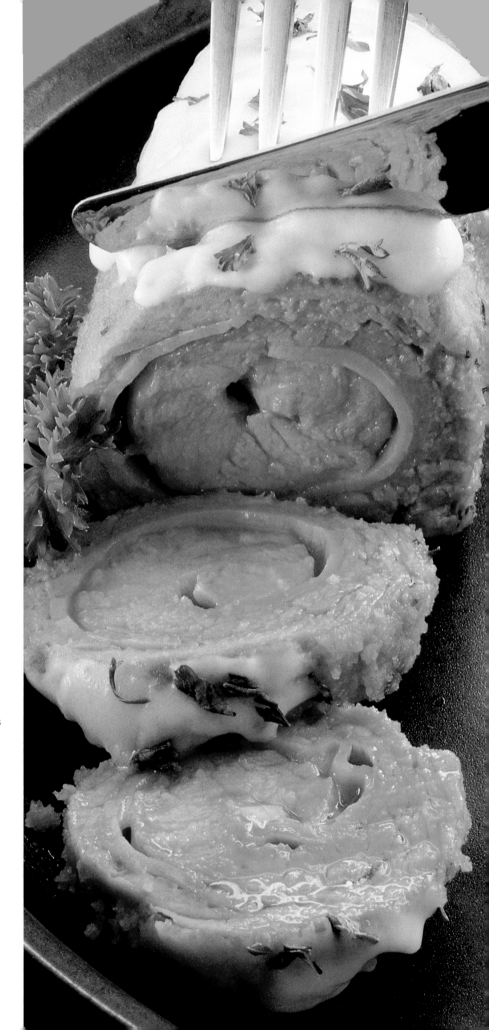

◄ Veal Italian

1 tablespoon all-purpose flour
1 tablespoon grated Parmesan
   cheese
⅛ teaspoon salt
   Dash pepper
¼ lb. veal boneless top round
   steak, cut into ½-in.
   strips, page 50
1 small tomato, chopped

1 tablespoon catsup
2 teaspoons sherry
⅛ teaspoon onion powder
⅛ teaspoon dried parsley flakes
⅛ teaspoon dried oregano
   leaves
   Dash dried basil leaves
¼ cup shredded mozzarella
   cheese

Serves 1

Combine flour, Parmesan cheese, salt and pepper in plastic bag. Shake meat in bag until coated. Arrange meat in 14-oz. oval individual casserole. In small bowl mix remaining ingredients except mozzarella. Spoon over meat. Cover with wax paper.

Microwave at 50% (Medium) 7 to 9 minutes, or until meat is tender and sauce is slightly thickened, stirring 2 or 3 times during cooking. Sprinkle with mozzarella cheese. Microwave at 50% (Medium) 1½ to 2 minutes, or until cheese melts.

Veal Italian for Two: Double all ingredients. Prepare as directed except use 1-qt. casserole. Microwave at 50% (Medium) 10 to 13 minutes. Sprinkle with mozzarella. Microwave 1½ to 2 minutes.

◄ Veal With Noodles & Cheese

2 tablespoons chopped onion
1 teaspoon butter or margarine
1 tablespoon all-purpose flour
½ teaspoon instant beef
   bouillon granules
¼ teaspoon dry mustard
⅛ teaspoon dried bouquet
   garni seasoning
⅛ teaspoon pepper
¼ lb. veal boneless bottom
   round steak, cut into
   ½-in. pieces, page 50

½ cup hot water
⅓ cup uncooked narrow egg
   noodles
¼ cup sliced fresh mushrooms
   or ½ can (2½ oz.) sliced
   mushrooms, drained
1 teaspoon dry vermouth
2 tablespoons shredded
   Cheddar cheese

Serves 1

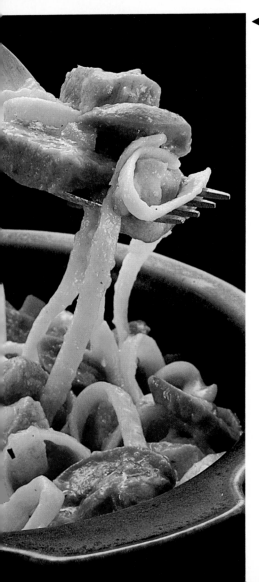

In 22-oz. individual casserole combine onion and butter. Microwave at High 1 to 2 minutes, or until onion is tender, stirring once. In plastic bag combine flour, bouillon granules, mustard, bouquet garni and pepper. Add meat, shaking to coat. Add meat to onion. Stir in water and noodles. Cover with wax paper.

Reduce power to 50% (Medium). Microwave 5 to 7 minutes, or until meat and noodles are tender, stirring after half the time. Stir in mushrooms and vermouth; cover. Microwave at 50% (Medium) 2 to 4 minutes, or until heated, stirring after half the time. Stir in cheese until melted. Let stand, covered, 3 minutes.

Veal With Noodles & Cheese for Two: Double all ingredients. Prepare as directed except use 1-qt. casserole or two 22-oz. individual casseroles. Microwave onion and butter at High 1 to 3 minutes. Reduce power to 50% (Medium). Microwave meat and noodles, covered, 10½ to 12½ minutes. Add mushrooms; microwave at 50% (Medium) 3 to 4½ minutes. After stirring in cheese, let stand, covered, 3 minutes.

Piquant Veal Chop ▲

¼ cup chopped tomato
2 tablespoons chili sauce
1 teaspoon packed brown
  sugar
⅛ teaspoon salt
  Dash dried basil leaves
1 veal loin chop, ⅓ to ½ lb.
2 green pepper rings, ¼-in.
  thick

Serves 1

Mix tomato, chili sauce, brown sugar, salt and basil. Place chop in 6¾ × 4½-in. individual casserole or 1-qt. square casserole. Pierce both sides with fork. Place green pepper rings on chop. Pour sauce over chop. Cover with wax paper. Microwave at 50% (Medium) 6 to 12 minutes, or until meat is cooked to desired tenderness, turning over and stirring sauce after half the cooking time.

Piquant Veal Chops for Two:
Double all ingredients. Prepare as directed except use 10 × 6-in. baking dish. Microwave at 50% (Medium) 10 to 15 minutes.

Hungarian Goulash

1 slice bacon, cut into ½-in.
  pieces
1 medium potato, cut into
  ½-in. cubes
⅓ cup chopped onion
¼ cup chopped green pepper
½ teaspoon caraway seed
1 teaspoon instant beef
  bouillon granules
¼ cup hot water
1 can (8 oz.) stewed
  tomatoes

½ teaspoon sugar
1 tablespoon plus 1½ tea-
  spoons all-purpose flour
½ teaspoon paprika
⅛ teaspoon pepper
½ lb. veal stew meat, ½-in.
  cubes
2 tablespoons dairy sour
  cream, optional

Serves 2

Place bacon in 1-qt. casserole. Microwave at High 45 to 60 seconds, or until brown. Stir in potato, onion, green pepper and caraway seed; cover. Microwave at High 7 to 9 minutes, or until onion and green pepper are tender. Dissolve bouillon granules in water. Stir into vegetables with tomatoes and sugar. Set aside. Mix flour, paprika and pepper. Toss with stew meat to coat; add to vegetables; cover.

Reduce power to 50% (Medium). Microwave 20 to 25 minutes, or until potatoes and meat are tender, stirring every 4 or 5 minutes. Top each serving with 1 tablespoon sour cream.

Hungarian Goulash for One: Refrigerate one serving no longer than 2 days. To reheat, microwave, covered, at 70% (Medium-High) 3 to 5 minutes, stirring after half the cooking time. Let stand, covered, 5 minutes.

◄ Veal With Carrots & Lemon

⅓ to ½-lb. veal boneless
   round steak
1 medium carrot, cut into
   1 × ⅛-in. strips
1½ teaspoons all-purpose flour
¼ teaspoon paprika
¼ teaspoon dried parsley
   flakes
⅛ teaspoon dried rosemary
   leaves
   Dash pepper
2 tablespoons white wine
1 tablespoon lemon juice
½ teaspoon instant beef
   bouillon granules

Serves 1

Pound both sides of veal steak with meat mallet. Cut into 1-in. pieces. Place carrots in 15-oz. individual casserole. Mix flour, paprika, parsley, rosemary and pepper. Toss with meat to coat. Arrange on carrots.

Mix wine, lemon juice and bouillon granules. Microwave at High 30 seconds. Stir until bouillon is dissolved. Stir into meat and carrots; cover. Reduce power to 50% (Medium). Microwave 14 to 17 minutes, or until carrots and meat are tender, stirring 2 or 3 times during cooking. If desired, serve over rice, page 133, and garnish with a lemon wedge.

Veal With Carrots & Lemon for Two: Double all ingredients. Prepare as directed except use 22-oz. casserole. Microwave at 50% (Medium) 18 to 24 minutes.

Tarragon Veal Steak ▲

¼ lb. veal boneless top round
   steak, page 50
1 teaspoon butter or margarine
1 teaspoon water
½ teaspoon white wine vinegar
⅛ teaspoon minced onion
⅛ teaspoon instant chicken
   bouillon granules
   Dash dried tarragon leaves
   Dash pepper
1 teaspoon all-purpose flour
1 tablespoon milk

Serves 1

Pound both sides of meat with edge of saucer or meat mallet. Place in 1-qt. square casserole. In 2-cup measure combine butter, water, vinegar, onion, bouillon granules, tarragon and pepper. Microwave at High 30 to 60 seconds, or until butter melts, stirring to dissolve bouillon. Pour over meat; cover. Reduce power to 50% (Medium). Microwave 1½ to 2½ minutes, or until veal is no longer pink outside but is slightly pink in center, turning over after half the time.

Remove meat to serving dish; stir flour into drippings. Gradually stir in milk. Increase power to High. Microwave 30 to 60 seconds, or until thickened, stirring once. Pour over meat.

Tarragon Veal Steaks for Two: Double all ingredients. Prepare as directed except microwave veal steaks at 50% (Medium) 2 to 3 minutes.

Mock City Chicken

¼ lb. ground veal
1 slice bacon, chopped
1 teaspoon chopped onion
1½ teaspoons snipped fresh
    parsley
⅛ teaspoon salt
⅛ teaspoon pepper
¼ teaspoon Worcestershire
    sauce
1 tablespoon plus 1½ tea-
    spoons beaten egg
2 tablespoons corn flake
    crumbs
1 popsicle stick

Serves 1

Mock City Chicken for Two:
Double all ingredients. Prepare
as directed except microwave
at High 5 to 6 minutes, rotating
and rearranging once.

How to Microwave Mock City Chicken

Combine veal, bacon, onion,
parsley, salt, pepper and
Worcestershire sauce.

Shape mixture into small, flat
loaf. Roll in beaten egg, then in
crumbs to coat.

Insert wooden stick through
loaf. Carefully place on roasting
rack. Cover with wax paper.

Microwave at High 3½ to 4½
minutes, or until meat is firm to
the touch and no longer pink,
rotating ½ turn after half the
time. Let stand 2 to 3 minutes.

Making the Most of Pork Loin

Boneless pork loin is a good buy for the small household. The cost per pound is higher than a bone-in roast, but you are not buying the bone, and the meat is easy to divide for several meals. Halve a 3-lb. boneless roast and set aside one piece for roast pork. From the other half, slice two chops, using about one-third of the piece. Cut the remaining pound of meat into strips and divide into two packages, each yielding two servings.

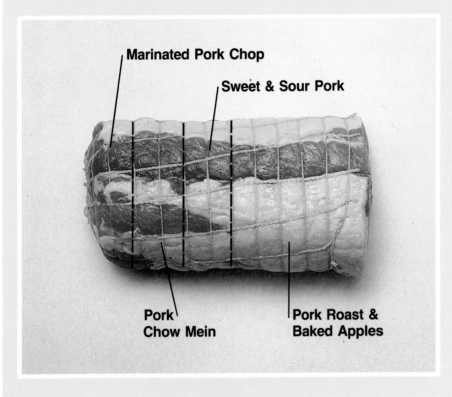

Marinated Pork Chop

Sweet & Sour Pork

Pork Chow Mein

Pork Roast & Baked Apples

Pork Roast & Baked Apples: Cut 1½-lb. pork boneless loin roast. Wrap, label and freeze no longer than 6 months. To defrost, microwave at 50% (Medium) 5 to 9 minutes, turning over after half the time and rotating every 3 minutes. If edges begin to cook, let stand to complete defrosting.

Marinated Pork Chop: Cut two ¼-lb. chops from ½-lb. pork loin. Wrap individually, label and freeze no longer than 4 months. To defrost, microwave one chop at 50% (Medium) 2½ to 4 minutes, turning over after each minute. If meat begins to cook around edges, let stand to complete defrosting.

Pork Chow Mein: Cut ½-lb. pork loin into 2 × ¼-in. strips. Wrap, label and freeze no longer than 4 months. To defrost, microwave at 50% (Medium) 3 to 4 minutes, breaking apart, removing any defrosted portions and turning over after half the time.

Sweet & Sour Pork: Cut ½-lb. pork loin into 2 × ¼-in. strips. Wrap, label and freeze no longer than 4 months. To defrost, microwave at 50% (Medium) 3 to 4 minutes, breaking apart, removing any defrosted portions and turning over after half the time.

Pork Roast & Baked Apples ▲

3 small apples, divided
¼ cup raisins
¼ cup maple syrup
2 tablespoons packed brown
   sugar
¼ teaspoon ground cinnamon
1½ lb. pork boneless loin roast,
   opposite

Serves 2

Core and chop one apple. In small bowl mix chopped apple, raisins, syrup, sugar and cinnamon. Stuff center of roast with half of fruit mixture. Place roast on roasting rack. Tie with butcher's string to secure stuffing.

Microwave at High 2 minutes. Reduce power to 50% (Medium). Microwave 10 minutes, rotating ¼ turn after half the time. Core remaining apples; place apples next to roast. Spoon remaining fruit mixture into apple centers. Baste roast with syrup from fruit mixture.

Microwave at 50% (Medium) 10 to 15 minutes, or until internal temperature of roast is 170°F. Check temperature in several places. Cover with foil. Let stand 10 minutes. Apples will tenderize after standing.

Pork Roast & Baked Apples for One: Wrap, label and freeze one serving no longer than 2 weeks. To defrost and heat, microwave at 50% (Medium) 6 to 12 minutes, turning over after half the time.

Marinated Pork Chop

1 boneless pork loin chop,
   ¼ lb., opposite
¼ cup sliced onion
2 tablespoons chili sauce
2 tablespoons white wine
½ teaspoon lemon juice
1 slice lemon
½ teaspoon packed brown
   sugar
⅛ teaspoon dried thyme leaves
⅛ teaspoon salt
   Dash pepper
   Dash garlic powder

Serves 1

Place meat in 1-qt. square casserole. Mix remaining ingredients; pour over meat. Refrigerate 3 hours.

Microwave, covered, at 50% (Medium) 25 to 30 minutes, or until tender and no longer pink, turning over after half the time.

Marinated Pork Chops for Two: Double all ingredients. Prepare as directed.

Pork Chow Mein ▲

½ lb. pork boneless loin, cut
   into 2 × ¼-in. strips, page 56
1 cup fresh or canned bean
   sprouts, drained
⅔ cup thinly sliced celery
½ cup sliced water chestnuts
1 can (2½ oz.) sliced
   mushrooms, drained
2 green onions, sliced

1 tablespoon sliced pimiento
2 teaspoons cornstarch
2 tablespoons soy sauce
2 tablespoons white wine
½ teaspoon instant chicken
   bouillon granules
1 teaspoon sugar
¼ teaspoon pepper

Serves 2

In 2-qt. casserole combine pork, bean sprouts, celery, water chestnuts, mushrooms, green onions and pimiento. Cover. Microwave at 50% (Medium) 14 to 17 minutes, or until meat is no longer pink and vegetables are tender, stirring 3 or 4 times. Drain liquid into 2-cup measure. Remove small amount of liquid and mix with cornstarch; return to cooking liquid in 2-cup measure. Cover pork and vegetables and set aside.

Add enough hot water to cooking liquid in 2-cup measure to measure ¾ cup. Stir in remaining ingredients. Increase power to High. Microwave 1½ to 3 minutes, or until thickened, stirring after first minute and then every 30 seconds. Pour over meat and vegetables; cover. Reduce power to 50% (Medium). Microwave 2 to 3 minutes, or until heated. Serve over chow mein noodles, if desired.

Pork Chow Mein for One: Wrap, label and freeze one serving no longer than 2 weeks. To defrost and heat, microwave at 70% (Medium-High) 6 to 9 minutes, stirring twice to break apart.

Sweet & Sour Pork ►

1 tablespoon vegetable oil
½ lb. pork boneless loin, cut
   into 2 × ¼-in. strips,
   page 56
1 medium carrot, thinly sliced
   or cut into thin strips
1 green onion, thinly sliced
¼ medium green pepper, cut
   into thin strips
1 can (8 oz.) chunk pineapple,
   drained, juice reserved
1 tablespoon packed brown
   sugar
1 tablespoon cornstarch
   Dash garlic powder
1 tablespoon cider vinegar
1 tablespoon soy sauce
2 teaspoons catsup
¼ cup cashews, optional

Serves 2

Preheat browning dish at High 5 minutes. Add oil; tilt dish to coat. Add pork. Reduce power to 50% (Medium). Microwave 2 to 3 minutes, or until no longer pink, stirring after half the time. Add vegetables. Cover with plastic wrap. Microwave at 50% (Medium) 7 to 9 minutes, or until vegetables are tender-crisp, stirring 3 times. Cover and set aside.

In 2-cup measure combine reserved pineapple juice, brown sugar, cornstarch, garlic powder, vinegar, soy sauce and catsup. Increase power to High. Microwave 2 to 3 minutes, or until clear and thick, stirring after the first minute and then every 30 seconds. Add thick-ened sauce and pineapple to meat and vegetables, tossing to coat. Serve over rice, page 133, if desired. Sprinkle with cashews.

Sweet & Sour Pork for One: Wrap, label and freeze one serving no longer than 2 weeks. To defrost and heat, microwave at 70% (Medium-High) 4 to 6 minutes, stirring twice during cooking to break apart.

Tamales ▶

4 cups hot water
4 dried corn husks

Filling:
¼ lb. pork boneless loin, cut
   into thin strips
1 medium tomato, chopped
¼ cup chopped onion
2 tablespoons chopped green
   chilies
2 tablespoons catsup
¼ teaspoon chili powder
⅛ teaspoon ground cumin
⅛ teaspoon dried basil leaves
⅛ teaspoon salt

Dough:
3 tablespoons butter or
   margarine
½ cup yellow cornmeal
½ teaspoon baking powder
   Dash salt
1 medium egg, slightly beaten
⅓ pkg. (3 oz.) cream cheese,
   softened
1 tablespoon honey

Serves 2

Tamales for One: Refrigerate
two tamales no longer than 2
days. To reheat, microwave at
50% (Medium) 1 to 3 minutes.

How to Microwave Tamales

Place hot water in large bowl.
Cover with plastic wrap. Microwave at High 8 to 10 minutes,
or until boiling. Place corn
husks in water; cover. Let stand.

Combine pork, tomato and
onion in 1-qt. casserole. Reduce
power to 50% (Medium).
Microwave 4 to 6 minutes, or
until meat is no longer pink,
stirring 3 times. Drain.

Add remaining filling ingredients
to pork. Microwave at 50%
(Medium) 4 to 6 minutes, or
until flavors blend and pork is
tender, stirring after half the
time. Set aside.

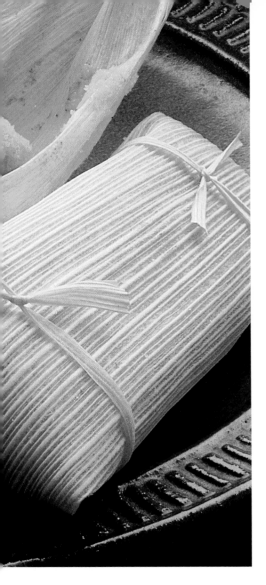

Corn Bread-Stuffed Pork Chop

2 slices bacon, cut into ½-in.
    pieces
1 small green onion, chopped
2 tablespoons chopped celery
¼ loaf corn bread, crumbled,
    page 137
2 teaspoons dried parsley
    flakes
⅛ teaspoon ground sage
¼ teaspoon salt, divided

⅛ teaspoon pepper, divided
1 pork boneless loin chop,
    1-in. thick, with pocket
2 tablespoons yellow cornmeal
2 tablespoons seasoned bread
    crumbs
⅛ teaspoon paprika
1 tablespoon butter or
    margarine
1 medium egg

Serves 1

Place bacon, onion and celery in 1-qt. casserole. Microwave at High 1½ to 2 minutes, or until bacon is light brown and vegetables are tender-crisp. Drain, reserving 2 tablespoons drippings in casserole. Add crumbled corn bread to bacon drippings, tossing to coat. Mix in parsley flakes, sage, ⅛ teaspoon salt and dash pepper. Stuff chop with half the stuffing mixture. Secure with wooden picks. Cover remaining stuffing; set aside.

In medium bowl combine cornmeal, bread crumbs, ⅛ teaspoon salt, the paprika and remaining dash pepper. Place butter in medium bowl. Microwave at High 30 to 45 seconds, or until melted. Beat egg into butter. Dip stuffed chop in egg mixture. Coat with crumb mixture, pressing meat lightly so crumbs adhere. Place chop on microwave roasting rack. Reduce power to 50% (Medium). Microwave 6 to 11 minutes, or until meat next to bone is no longer pink, turning over after half the cooking time. Serve with remaining stuffing.

Corn Bread-Stuffed Pork Chops for Two: Double all ingredients. Prepare as directed except microwave bacon and vegetables at High 3½ to 4 minutes. Reduce power to 50% (Medium). Microwave chops 8 to 12 minutes, turning over and rotating after half the time.

Place butter in small bowl or 2-cup measure. Increase power to High. Microwave 30 to 45 seconds, or until butter melts. Stir in remaining dough ingredients until blended.

Spread one-fourth of dough mixture down center of each husk. Top with one-fourth of filling, spreading to within ¼ inch of dough. Roll husks around filling. Secure ends with string. Arrange tamales in 8 × 8-in. baking dish.

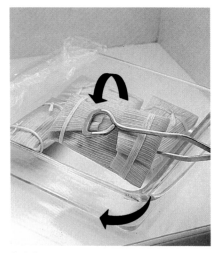

Add 1 teaspoon water to dish. Cover with plastic wrap. Reduce power to 50% (Medium). Microwave 3 to 6 minutes, or until firm to the touch, turning tamales over and rotating dish after half the time.

Vegetable
Braised Spareribs

¾ lb. fresh pork country-style
    spareribs
½ cup plus 2 tablespoons hot
    water, divided
1 new potato, peeled
    and grated
½ medium tomato, cut into
    ¼-in. slices
½ cup shredded cabbage,
    page 124
¼ cup sliced onion
¼ teaspoon instant beef
    bouillon granules
    Dash dried basil leaves
    Dash salt
    Dash pepper
1 teaspoon bouquet sauce
1 teaspoon water

Serves 1

Place spareribs and ½ cup
water in 1-qt. casserole; cover.
Microwave at 50% (Medium) 9
to 12 minutes, or until meat is
no longer pink, stirring once or
twice. Drain; set aside.

Combine potato, tomato, cabbage and onion in 8 × 8-in.
baking dish or 1-qt. square
casserole. Dissolve bouillon
granules in 2 tablespoons hot
water. Pour over vegetables.
Sprinkle with basil, salt and
pepper. Mix bouquet sauce and
1 teaspoon water; brush over
spareribs. Add spareribs to
vegetables; cover. Microwave at
50% (Medium) 25 to 30 minutes, or until meat is fork tender,
turning meat over and stirring
vegetables every 10 minutes.
Let stand, covered, 5 minutes.

**Vegetable Braised Spareribs
for Two:** Double all ingredients.
Prepare as directed except use
2-qt. casserole. Microwave
spareribs and water at 50%
(Medium) 16 to 19 minutes.
Microwave vegetables and
spareribs at 50% (Medium) 33
to 38 minutes.

Vegetable-Stuffed Pork Tenderloin ▲

1 cup white wine
2 tablespoons apple jelly
1 tablespoon chopped onion
2 slices fresh lemon
3 whole cloves
1 clove garlic, minced
½ teaspoon dried tarragon
    leaves

½ to ¾-lb. pork tenderloin
3 slices bacon
1 teaspoon butter or margarine
1 carrot, cut into long thin
    strips
1 green onion, cut into 4 thin
    strips

Serves 2

In 10 × 6-in. baking dish mix wine, apple jelly, onion, lemon slices,
cloves, garlic and tarragon. Microwave at High 2 to 3 minutes, or
until heated, stirring to dissolve jelly after half the time. Form pocket
in tenderloin by cutting lengthwise down center to within ½ inch of
bottom. Open up and place in baking dish with wine marinade;
cover. Refrigerate 1 hour.

Place bacon on paper towel-lined plate. Microwave at High 1 to
1½ minutes, or until light brown, but not crisp. Place butter, carrot
and onion strips in 1-qt. casserole; cover. Microwave at High 1½ to
2½ minutes, or until tender, stirring after half the time.

Remove roast from marinade. Place vegetables in the center cut.
Close center, securing with wooden picks. Wrap bacon pieces
around roast, securing with wooden picks. Place on roasting rack.
Reduce power to 50% (Medium). Microwave 11 to 16 minutes, or
until internal temperature is 170°F., rotating roast 2 or 3 times
during cooking. Check temperature in several places.

Vegetable-Stuffed Pork Tenderloin for One: Refrigerate one
serving no longer than 2 days. To reheat, microwave at 70%
(Medium-High) 1½ to 3 minutes.

Barbecued Spareribs

¾ lb. fresh pork country-style
    spareribs
½ cup water
1 tablespoon plus 1½ tea-
    spoons butter or margarine
1 tablespoon chopped onion
1 small clove garlic, minced
¼ cup catsup
2 tablespoons chili sauce
1½ teaspoons Worcestershire
    sauce
½ teaspoon prepared mustard
1 thin slice lemon or ½
    teaspoon lemon juice
½ teaspoon celery salt
⅛ teaspoon salt
    Dash red pepper sauce

Serves 1

Place spareribs and water in
1-qt. casserole; cover.
Microwave at 50% (Medium) 9
to 12 minutes, or until meat is
no longer pink, stirring once or
twice. Drain; set aside.

In 4-cup measure place butter,
onion and garlic; cover. Increase power to High. Microwave 1½ to 2 minutes, or until
onion is tender, stirring after half
the time. Stir in remaining ingredients. Microwave at High 2 to
3 minutes, or until hot and
bubbly, stirring once.

Place spareribs on roasting
rack. Remove lemon slice from
sauce. Brush spareribs with half
the sauce. Reduce power to
50% (Medium). Microwave 8 to
10 minutes, or until spareribs
are fork tender, turning over and
basting with remaining sauce
after half the cooking time.

Barbecued Spareribs for Two:
Double all ingredients. Prepare
as directed except microwave
spareribs in water at 50%
(Medium) 16 to 19 minutes.
Increase power to High. Microwave butter, onion and garlic 2
to 3 minutes; sauce 3 to 4 minutes. Reduce power to 50%
(Medium). Finish ribs for 10 to
13 minutes.

Orange-Glazed Ham ▲

1 tablespoon packed brown
    sugar
⅛ teaspoon ground ginger
½ teaspoon grated orange peel

1 orange slice, ¼-in. thick
¼ cup orange juice
¼ lb. fully cooked ham slice,
    about ½-in. thick

Serves 1

In 10 × 6-in. baking dish mix brown sugar, ginger, orange peel,
orange slice and orange juice. Place ham in dish, turning over to
coat with sauce; cover. Let stand 30 minutes.

Preheat browning dish at High 5 minutes. Place ham in browning
dish; press down. Turn over; press down again. Microwave at High
1 to 2 minutes, or until light brown, turning over after half the time.
Pour sauce over ham. Reduce power to 50% (Medium). Microwave
4 to 6 minutes, or until sauce and ham are heated, basting after
half the time. Remove ham to serving plate.

If desired, thicken sauce by stirring in ½ teaspoon cornstarch.
Microwave at High 1 to 2 minutes, stirring after half the time.

Orange-Glazed Ham for Two: Use two ham slices, but same
amount of sauce ingredients. Prepare as directed.

Honey-Rum Ham Slice

¼ cup dark rum
2 teaspoons honey
1 teaspoon Dijon-style mustard
6 whole cloves
¼ lb. fully cooked ham slice,
    about ½-in. thick

Serves 1

In 10 × 6-in. baking dish mix rum,
honey, mustard and cloves.
Place ham in dish, turning over
to coat with sauce; cover. Let
stand 30 minutes. Preheat
browning dish at High 5 minutes. Place ham in browning
dish; press down. Turn over;
press down again. Microwave
at High 1 to 2 minutes, or until
light brown, turning over after
half the time. Pour sauce over
ham. Reduce power to 50%
(Medium). Microwave 4 to 6
minutes, or until heated, basting
after half the time.

**Honey-Rum Ham Slice for
Two:** Use two ham slices, but
same amount of sauce ingredients. Prepare as directed.

64

Ham-Stuffed Cabbage Rolls

2 cabbage leaves, page 124
¼ cup hot water, divided
2 tablespoons uncooked
    instant rice
½ cup diced fully cooked ham
⅛ lb. ground pork
1 tablespoon plus 1½
    teaspoons beaten egg
1½ teaspoons minced onion

⅛ teaspoon dry mustard,
    divided
Dash salt
Dash pepper
1 small tomato, cut into
    8 wedges
1 tablespoon chili sauce
½ teaspoon packed brown
    sugar

Serves 1

Ham-Stuffed Cabbage Rolls for Two: Double all ingredients. Prepare as directed except microwave water for rice at High 45 to 60 seconds. Microwave cabbage leaves at High 3½ to 4½ minutes. Place cabbage rolls in 1-qt. square casserole. Reduce power to 50% (Medium). Microwave 11 to 13 minutes.

How to Microwave Ham-Stuffed Cabbage Rolls

Remove two outer leaves from cabbage head as directed. Place remainder of head in plastic bag and refrigerate for other use. Cut out hard center rib from each leaf.

Place 2 tablespoons hot water in small bowl. Cover with plastic wrap. Microwave at High 30 to 45 seconds, or until boiling. Stir in rice. Cover and let stand.

Place cabbage leaves and 2 tablespoons hot water in 1-qt. casserole; cover. Microwave at High 2 to 3 minutes, or until tender, turning leaves over after half the time. Set aside.

Mix ham, ground pork, egg, onion, dash mustard, the salt, pepper and cooked rice in medium bowl. Place half of meat mixture in center of each cabbage leaf.

Roll sides around meat. Place rolls seam side down in 6¾ × 4½-in. individual casserole. Top with tomato. In small bowl mix chili sauce, brown sugar and remaining dash mustard.

Pour over cabbage rolls; cover. Reduce power to 50% (Medium). Microwave 6 to 8 minutes, or until rolls are firm to the touch and internal temperature is 160°F., rotating twice.

65

Ham Loaf

　1 pineapple slice

Loaf:

　⅛ lb. ground ham
　⅛ lb. ground pork
　1 tablespoon saltine cracker
　　crumbs
　1 tablespoon plus 1½ tea-
　　spoons slightly beaten egg
1½ teaspoons chopped green
　　onion
1½ teaspoons chopped green
　　pepper
1½ teaspoons snipped fresh
　　parsley
　⅛ teaspoon salt
　　Dash pepper
　　Dash dried thyme leaves

Sauce:

1½ teaspoons packed brown
　　sugar
　¼ teaspoon prepared mustard
　¼ teaspoon cider vinegar
　⅛ teaspoon cornstarch

Serves 1

Place pineapple slice in 6½ × 4-in. loaf dish. Mix all loaf ingredients in medium bowl. Shape into loaf. Place on top of pineapple slice.

Microwave at 50% (Medium) 8 to 10½ minutes, or until center is no longer pink, and internal temperature reaches 160°F., rotating dish every 3 minutes. Drain drippings into 1-cup measure. Add enough water to drippings to measure 1 table-spoon. Stir sauce ingredients into drippings. Increase power to High. Microwave sauce 30 to 60 seconds, or until clear and thickened, stirring after half the time. Pour sauce over loaf.

Ham Loaf for Two: Double all ingredients. Prepare as directed except shape into two loaves. Microwave loaves at 50% (Medium) 10 to 14 minutes. Increase power to High. Microwave sauce 45 seconds to 1¼ minutes.

Ham Roll-Ups ▲

　1 tablespoon plus 1½ tea-
　　spoons butter or margarine
　1 tablespoon chopped onion
　　Dash salt
　　Dash pepper
1½ teaspoons all-purpose flour
　¼ cup milk

　¼ cup shredded Cheddar
　　cheese, divided
　½ cup diced fully cooked ham
　¼ cup frozen chopped
　　broccoli, defrosted
　　Dash nutmeg
　½ sheet lefse, cut in half, or 2
　　crêpes

Serves 1

Place butter, onion, salt and pepper in 2-cup measure. Microwave at High 30 to 45 seconds, or until butter melts and onion is tender. Stir in flour. Blend in milk. Microwave at High 30 to 60 seconds, or until thickened, stirring every 30 seconds. Stir in 3 tablespoons cheese until melted. Remove 1 tablespoon cheese sauce for topping. Add ham, broccoli and nutmeg to remaining sauce.

To assemble rolls, spoon half of ham-broccoli mixture down the center of each piece of lefse. Roll up, starting with pointed end. Fold ends under. Place in 6¾ × 4½-in. individual casserole. Top with reserved sauce and sprinkle with remaining 1 tablespoon cheese. Reduce power to 50% (Medium). Microwave 2 to 3 minutes, or until rolls are heated and cheese melts.

Ham Roll-Ups for Two: Double all ingredients. Prepare as directed except microwave sauce at High 1 to 2 minutes. Reduce power to 50% (Medium). Microwave roll-ups 2½ to 3½ minutes.

Ham Tetrazzini

½ serving spaghetti, page 131
2 tablespoons butter or
    margarine, divided
1 teaspoon grated Parmesan
    cheese
1 teaspoon dried parsley flakes
2 tablespoons chopped onion
1 tablespoon all-purpose flour
½ cup half and half
½ teaspoon prepared
    horseradish
⅛ teaspoon salt
    Dash pepper
½ cup fully cooked ham strips,
    2 × ¼-in.
2 tablespoons shredded
    Cheddar cheese
½ can (2½ oz.) sliced mush-
    rooms (about 2 tablespoons)
2 tablespoons slivered
    almonds

Serves 1

Prepare spaghetti as directed.
In small bowl toss spaghetti with
1 tablespoon butter, the
Parmesan cheese and parsley
flakes. Set aside.

Place 1 tablespoon butter and
the onion in 1-qt. casserole or
4-cup measure. Microwave at
High 1½ to 2½ minutes, or until
onion is tender, stirring after half
the time. Stir in flour. Gradually
stir in half and half. Add
horseradish, salt and pepper.
Microwave at High 1 to 2
minutes, or until thickened,
stirring every 30 seconds. Add
ham, Cheddar cheese,
mushrooms and almonds. Pour
over spaghetti in serving dish.
Reduce power to 50%
(Medium). Microwave 4 to 6
minutes, or until heated.

Ham Tetrazzini for Two:
Double all ingredients. Prepare
as directed except microwave
onion and butter at High 3 to 4
minutes; sauce mixture at High
2 to 3 minutes. Add remaining
ingredients. Reduce power to
50% (Medium). Microwave 5 to
7 minutes.

Ham Boats ▲

1 baking potato
2 tablespoons milk
2 tablespoons dairy sour
    cream
½ cup fully cooked ham strips,
    2 × ¼-in.

1 tablespoon chopped green
    onion
⅛ teaspoon dry mustard
2 tablespoons shredded
    Cheddar cheese

Serves 1

Pierce potato with fork 2 or 3 times. Place in oven on paper towel.
Microwave at High 3 to 5 minutes, or until soft to the touch, turning
over after half the time. Wrap in foil or place under inverted bowl;
let stand 5 minutes.

Slice potato in half lengthwise. Scoop out center. Set shells aside.
Mash potato center with milk and sour cream. Mix in ham, green
onion and mustard. Spoon into potato shells. Sprinkle 1 tablespoon
cheese on each. Reduce power to 50% (Medium). Microwave 3 to
4 minutes, or until cheese melts and potato is heated.

Ham Boats for Two: Double all ingredients. Prepare as directed
except microwave potatoes at High 5 to 7½ minutes. Reduce
power to 50% (Medium). Microwave filled potato shells 4 to
5 minutes.

◄ Seasoned Rack of Lamb

1 single rack of lamb, cut in
   half and rib ends exposed
2 cloves garlic, cut in half
¼ teaspoon dried rosemary
   leaves

¼ teaspoon dried oregano
   leaves
¼ teaspoon dried marjoram
   leaves

Serves 2

**Seasoned Rack of Lamb for
One:** Wrap, label and freeze
one serving, trimmed of excess
fat, no longer than 4 weeks. To
defrost and heat, microwave at
50% (Medium) 6 to 9 minutes.

Desired Doneness	Removal Temp.
Rare	120°F.
Medium	135°F.
Well	150°F.

How to Microwave Seasoned Rack of Lamb

Stand rack halves on backbone
edges, concave sides facing
each other; press together.
Interlace bone ends.

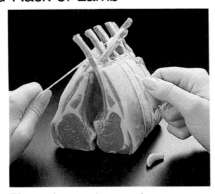

Tie rack together and weave
around crossed ribs with
butchers' string. Rub surface of
roast with half clove garlic.

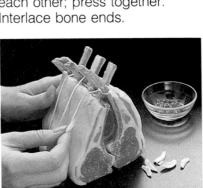

Cut three lengthwise slits, ¼
inch deep, in outer surface on
each side of roast. Cut
remaining garlic into slivers and
place in slits. Mix rosemary,
oregano and marjoram. Rub
lightly onto all surfaces.

Place on roasting rack.
Microwave at 50% (Medium) 11
to 15 minutes, or until desired
doneness, turning ¼ turn every
2 minutes. Cover with foil and
let stand 10 minutes.

Lamb Chop With Orange

½ medium orange
1 teaspoon packed brown
   sugar
1 teaspoon dry red wine
2 whole cloves
   Dash nutmeg
1 lamb shoulder chop, ½-lb.
½ teaspoon cornstarch

Serves 1

Cut two slices from orange half.
Squeeze 1 tablespoon juice into
2-cup measure from remainder
of orange section. Add brown
sugar, wine, cloves and nutmeg
to juice. Microwave at High 30
to 60 seconds, or until heated.
Stir to dissolve sugar.

Place lamb chop in 1-qt.
casserole or 6½-in. glass skillet.
Pour orange mixture over; top
with orange slices. Cover with
wax paper. Reduce power to
50% (Medium). Microwave 5½
to 8 minutes, or until desired
doneness, turning chop over
and stirring juice after half the
cooking time.

Discard cloves; remove chop
and orange slices to serving
dish. Stir cornstarch into
drippings in skillet. Increase
power to High. Microwave 30 to
60 seconds, or until slightly
thickened, stirring after half the
time. Pour over chop to serve.

**Lamb Chops With Orange for
Two:** Double all ingredients.
Prepare as directed except
microwave chops at 50%
(Medium) 8½ to 10½ minutes.
Increase power to High. Micro-
wave sauce 1 to 2 minutes.

Lamb Almondine ▲

1 teaspoon all-purpose flour
½ teaspoon dried parsley flakes
⅛ teaspoon salt
  Dash pepper
2 tablespoons sherry
1 lamb shoulder chop, ½-lb.
1 tablespoon sliced almonds
1 teaspoon butter or margarine
1 tablespoon dairy sour cream

Serves 1

In 1-qt. square casserole mix flour, parsley, salt, pepper and sherry. Place chop in casserole, turning over to coat with sherry mixture; cover. Microwave at 50% (Medium) 11 to 15 minutes, or until tender, turning over after half the time. Cover; set aside.

Place almonds and butter in small dish. Increase power to High. Microwave 3 to 4 minutes, or until light brown, tossing with fork after each minute. Place chop on serving plate. Stir almonds and sour cream into drippings in casserole. Reduce power to 50% (Medium). Microwave 1 to 2 minutes, or until heated, stirring after half the time. Spoon over meat.

Lamb Almondine for Two:
Double all ingredients. Prepare as directed except microwave at 50% (Medium) 20 to 28 minutes, turning over and rotating 2 or 3 times. Increase power to High. Microwave almonds 3 to 4 minutes. Reduce power to 50% (Medium). Microwave sauce 2 to 3½ minutes.

Bacon-Wrapped Chops

1 teaspoon butter or
  margarine
½ can (2½ oz.) sliced mushrooms, drained, chopped
2 tablespoons bread crumbs
⅛ teaspoon dried parsley
  flakes
⅛ teaspoon salt
  Dash dried marjoram leaves
  Dash garlic powder
2 lamb loin chops, 1-in. thick
2 slices bacon

Serves 1

Melt butter in small dish at High 30 to 45 seconds. Mix with mushrooms, bread crumbs, parsley, salt, marjoram, and garlic powder. Make a slit in the meaty side of each chop and stuff each with half of mush-room mixture, pressing in firmly with fingers. Secure with wooden picks.

Place bacon on paper towel in oven. Microwave at High 1 to 1½ minutes, or until light brown but not crisp. Wrap one slice bacon around meaty side of each chop; secure with wooden picks. Arrange bone side in on roasting rack. Microwave at High 3 to 5½ minutes, or until lamb is desired doneness, turning over after half the time.

Bacon-Wrapped Chops for Two: Double all ingredients. Prepare as directed except microwave bacon at High 2½ to 3½ minutes and chops at High 5½ to 7 minutes.

Lamb Sandwiches

1 lb. lamb shank
¾ cup hot water
1 envelope (single-serving
  size) dry onion soup mix
¼ teaspoon garlic powder
⅛ teaspoon caraway seed
⅛ teaspoon pepper
1 tablespoon all-purpose flour
¼ teaspoon bouquet sauce
1 large sandwich bun

Serves 2

Place lamb shank in 8 × 8-in. baking dish. Combine hot water, onion soup mix, garlic powder, caraway seed and pepper. Pour over lamb. Cover with plastic wrap. Microwave at 50% (Medium) 40 to 50 minutes, or until fork tender, turning and basting shank 3 or 4 times during cooking.

Remove lamb. Set aside, covered. Skim fat from liquid; pour liquid into 2-cup measure. Stir in flour and bouquet sauce. Increase power to High. Micro-wave 1 to 1½ minutes, or until thickened, stirring once.

Remove meat from bone; shred or cut meat into small pieces. Combine meat with sauce. Spoon into large sandwich bun. Wrap in paper towel. Microwave at High 15 to 30 seconds, or until bun is warm.

Lamb Sandwich for One:
Refrigerate half the meat mixture no longer than 2 days. To reheat, microwave at 70% (Medium-High) 1½ to 3 minutes, stirring after half the time.

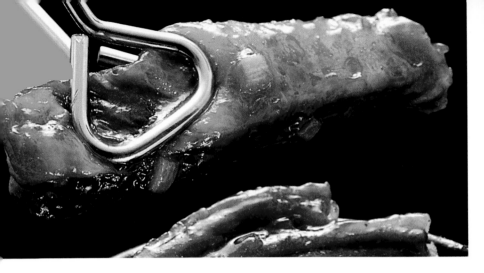

Orange-Barbecue Riblets ▲

¾ lb. lamb riblets
⅛ teaspoon pepper
2 tablespoons orange juice,
  divided
2 tablespoons catsup
1 tablespoon chopped onion
1 tablespoon packed brown
  sugar
1½ teaspoons cider vinegar
¼ teaspoon salt
⅛ teaspoon Worcestershire
  sauce
  Dash garlic powder
1 or 2 drops liquid smoke

Serves 1

Arrange riblets in 8 × 8-in. baking dish. Sprinkle with pepper
and 1 tablespoon orange juice;
cover. Microwave at High 5 to 7
minutes, or until riblets are no
longer pink, rearranging after
half the cooking time. Drain.
Place riblets on roasting rack.

Mix remaining 1 tablespoon
orange juice with all remaining
ingredients; pour over riblets.
Reduce power to 50%
(Medium). Microwave 10 to 13
minutes, or until tender.

**Orange-Barbecue Riblets for
Two:** Double all ingredients.
Prepare as directed except
microwave riblets at High 6 to 8
minutes. Reduce power to 50%
(Medium). Finish ribs for 14
to 16 minutes.

Greek Kabob ►

2 tablespoons olive oil
3 thin lemon slices
¼ teaspoon garlic powder
¼ teaspoon ground ginger
¼ teaspoon dried mint leaves
  Few drops red pepper sauce
¼ lb. lamb boneless shoulder,
  cut into 1-in. cubes
1 wooden skewer, 10-in. long
2 colossal pitted black olives
½ small onion, cut in half
3 large cherry tomatoes

Serves 1

In small bowl combine olive oil,
lemon slices, garlic powder,
ginger, mint leaves and red
pepper sauce. Microwave at
High 30 to 60 seconds, or until
lamb is heated and lemon is
tender. Add lamb cubes to
bowl; cover. Marinate at room
temperature 1 hour.

On wooden skewer, alternate
remaining ingredients with lamb,
beginning and ending with an
olive and onion quarter. Place
on roasting rack. Cover with
wax paper.

Reduce power to 50%
(Medium). Microwave 2 to 4
minutes, or until lamb is desired
doneness, turning over after half
the time.

Greek Kabobs for Two:
Double all ingredients. Prepare
as directed except microwave
kabobs at 50% (Medium) 4½ to
6 minutes.

Moussaka ▲

¼ lb. ground lamb
1 new potato, peeled and cut
  into ¼-in. cubes
½ cup chopped tomato
¼ cup cubed peeled egg-
  plant, ½-in. cubes
½ teaspoon snipped fresh
  parsley, divided
⅛ teaspoon plus dash salt,
  divided
⅛ teaspoon pepper, divided

Dash dried basil leaves
1½ teaspoons catsup
2 teaspoons butter or
  margarine, divided
1 teaspoon all-purpose flour
2 tablespoons milk
¼ cup cottage cheese
1 tablespoon grated
  Parmesan cheese
1 tablespoon dried bread
  crumbs

Serves 1

Crumble ground lamb into 22-oz. individual casserole. Stir in potato, tomato, eggplant, ¼ teaspoon parsley, ⅛ teaspoon salt, dash pepper and the basil; cover with wax paper. Microwave at High 8 to 10 minutes, or until lamb is no longer pink and potatoes are tender, stirring once during cooking to break lamb apart. Drain. Stir in catsup.

Place 1 teaspoon butter in 2-cup measure. Microwave at High 15 to 30 seconds, or until melted. Stir in flour, remaining dash salt and dash pepper. Blend in milk. Microwave at High 30 to 60 seconds, or until thickened, stirring after half the time. Blend in cottage cheese and Parmesan cheese. Spread over lamb mixture.

Place remaining 1 teaspoon butter in small dish. Microwave at High 15 to 30 seconds, or until melted. Add bread crumbs and remaining ¼ teaspoon parsley, tossing to coat. Sprinkle over cheese layer. Cover with wax paper. Reduce power to 50% (Medium). Microwave 2 to 3½ minutes, or until cheese is melted and set. Let stand 3 to 5 minutes.

Moussaka for Two: Double all ingredients. Prepare as directed except use 1-qt. casserole to microwave seasoned meat and vegetables. Divide between two 22-oz. individual casseroles. Melt first butter at High 30 to 45 seconds; thicken sauce at High 1 to 1½ minutes; melt butter at High 30 to 45 seconds. Reduce power to 50% (Medium). Melt cheese 5 to 7 minutes.

Lamb Curry ▲

¼ lb. lamb boneless stew meat,
  cut into ½-in. pieces
1 tablespoon chopped onion
½ cup hot water
2 tablespoons uncooked long
  grain rice
2 tablespoons raisins
2 tablespoons chopped celery
¼ teaspoon instant chicken
  bouillon granules
¼ teaspoon salt
¼ teaspoon curry powder
⅛ teaspoon ground ginger

Serves 1

Place meat and onion in 1-qt. casserole; cover. Microwave at High 1 to 1½ minutes, or until meat is no longer pink, stirring once. Drain. Stir in remaining ingredients. Cover. Reduce power to 50% (Medium). Microwave 14 to 16 minutes, or until rice and meat are tender, stirring 3 or 4 times during cooking. If desired, top serving with chopped hard cooked egg, crumbled crisp bacon, chopped peanuts, flaked coconut or chopped green onion.

Lamb Curry for Two: Double all ingredients. Prepare as directed except use 1½-qt. casserole. Microwave meat and onion at High 2 to 3 minutes. Reduce power to 50% (Medium). Microwave 14 to 16 minutes.

Lamb Patty

¼ lb. ground lamb
1½ teaspoons finely chopped
    onion
⅛ teaspoon salt
    Dash garlic powder
⅛ teaspoon dried marjoram
    leaves, dried mint flakes
    or ground ginger
    Mustard Topping, Mint Jelly
    Topping or Chutney
    Topping, below

Serves 1

Combine ground lamb, onion, salt and garlic powder. Add marjoram if using Mustard Topping, mint if using Mint Jelly Topping or ginger if using Chutney Topping. Mix well; shape into ½-in. thick patty.

Preheat browning dish at High 5 minutes. Place patty in dish. Microwave at High 30 seconds. Turn over. Microwave at High 30 to 60 seconds, or until lamb is medium-well done.

Or place patty on roasting rack. Microwave at High 1½ minutes. Turn over. Microwave at High 1 to 1½ minutes. Spread with one of the toppings.

Lamb Patties for Two: Double all ingredients. Prepare as directed except shape into two patties. In browning dish, microwave first side at High 1 minute; second side at High 1 to 2 minutes. On roasting rack, microwave first side at High 2 minutes; second side at High 1½ to 2½ minutes. Double topping ingredients.

Toppings:
Mustard Topping: Mix 1 tablespoon mayonnaise or salad dressing, ¼ teaspoon dry mustard and dash red pepper sauce.

Mint Jelly Topping: Stir 1 teaspoon mint apple or currant jelly until smooth.

Chutney Topping: Mix 1 tablespoon chutney and 1 teaspoon lemon juice.

Lamb With Kidney Beans ▲

Meatballs:
¼ cup hot water
2 tablespoons uncooked
    bulgur wheat
½ lb. ground lamb
1 tablespoon chopped onion
¼ teaspoon ground cumin
¼ teaspoon dried marjoram
    leaves
¼ teaspoon dried parsley flakes
¼ teaspoon salt

Sauce:
¼ cup coarsely chopped green
    pepper
1 tablespoon chopped onion
¼ teaspoon salt
2 or 3 drops red pepper sauce
1 teaspoon olive oil
1 can (8 oz.) kidney beans,
    drained
1 can (8 oz.) stewed tomatoes

Serves 2

Place hot water in 1-cup measure; cover. Microwave at High 45 to 60 seconds, or until boiling. Stir in bulgur. Let stand 1 hour. Drain any excess water. Mix all remaining meatball ingredients with bulgur. Shape into six meatballs. Arrange around sides of 1½- to 2-qt. casserole. Cover with wax paper. Microwave at High 1½ to 2 minutes, or until meat is no longer pink, turning over after half the time. Drain.

In small bowl combine green pepper, onion, salt, red pepper sauce and olive oil; cover. Microwave at High 2 to 4 minutes, or until tender, stirring after half the time. Stir into meat with kidney beans and stewed tomatoes; cover. Reduce power to 50% (Medium). Microwave 8 to 11 minutes, or until meatballs are firm to the touch and mixture is heated through, stirring after half the time.

Lamb With Kidney Beans for One: Wrap, label and freeze one serving no longer than 2 weeks. To defrost and heat, microwave at 70% (Medium-High) 7 to 9 minutes, stirring twice during cooking.

◀ Bologna & Potato Salad

¼ teaspoon salt, divided
¼ cup hot water
3 new potatoes, cut into ½-in. cubes
2 tablespoons mayonnaise or salad dressing
1 teaspoon snipped fresh parsley
2 teaspoons Dijon-style mustard
½ teaspoon vinegar
¼ teaspoon sugar
⅛ teaspoon dill weed
Dash pepper
1 lb. ring bologna

Serves 2

In 1-qt. casserole dissolve ⅛ teaspoon salt in hot water. Add potatoes; cover. Microwave at High 5 to 7 minutes, or until fork tender, stirring after half the cooking time. Drain.

In small bowl combine mayonnaise, parsley, mustard, vinegar, sugar, dill weed, remaining ⅛ teaspoon salt and the pepper. Stir in potatoes. Place bologna in 7-in. pie plate.

Cut bologna diagonally every 2 inches to ¼-in. depth. Place potato salad in center of ring. Cover with wax paper. Reduce power to 50% (Medium). Microwave 7 to 9 minutes, or until heated, rotating ½ turn twice during cooking.

Bologna & Potato Salad for One: Refrigerate one serving no longer than 2 days. To reheat, microwave at 50% (Medium) 5 to 7 minutes, rotating dish twice during cooking time.

Creole Sausage ▲

¼ lb. sweet Italian sausage
2 tablespoons chopped celery
2 tablespoons chopped green
   pepper
2 tablespoons chopped green
   onion
1 can (8 oz.) stewed tomatoes
1 tablespoon catsup
2 teaspoons all-purpose flour
½ teaspoon sugar
¼ teaspoon chili powder
⅛ teaspoon paprika
⅛ teaspoon pepper
⅛ teaspoon cayenne pepper

Serves 2

Crumble sausage into 1-qt. casserole. Add celery, green pepper and green onion. Cover with wax paper. Microwave at High 4 to 5 minutes, or until meat is no longer pink and vegetables are tender, stirring after half the time to break apart. Drain.

Stir in remaining ingredients. Reduce power to 50% (Medium). Cover with wax paper. Microwave 7 to 9 minutes, or until slightly thickened and flavors blend. Serve over rice, page 133, if desired.

Creole Sausage for One:
Refrigerate one serving no longer than 2 days. To reheat, microwave at 70% (Medium-High) 3 to 4 minutes, stirring after half the time.

Kielbasa & Cheese Spaghetti

½ serving spaghetti,
   page 131
1½ teaspoons butter or
   margarine
   Dash garlic powder
   Dash dried basil leaves
⅛ teaspoon snipped fresh
   parsley
1 tablespoon grated Romano
   cheese
1 fully cooked Polish
   (kielbasa) sausage

Serves 1

Prepare spaghetti as directed. Add butter, garlic powder, basil, parsley and Romano cheese. Toss to coat. Arrange spaghetti in 14-oz. oval individual casserole. If desired, score sausage diagonally at 1-in. intervals. Place on top of spaghetti. Cover with wax paper. Microwave at High 45 to 60 seconds, or until heated, rotating once.

Kielbasa & Cheese Spaghetti for Two: Double all ingredients. Prepare as directed except use 9-in. pie plate or serving dish. Microwave at High 1½ to 2 minutes, rotating once.

Sausage & Kraut Stuffing

¼ lb. unseasoned bulk pork
   sausage
1 small onion, thinly sliced
¼ cup chopped celery
1 can (8 oz.) sauerkraut,
   drained and rinsed
1 small apple, chopped
2 teaspoons packed brown
   sugar
½ teaspoon white vinegar
¼ teaspoon caraway seed
   Dash pepper

Makes 2 cups

Place sausage, onion, and celery in 1- to 1½-qt. casserole; cover. Microwave at High 4 to 5 minutes, or until sausage is no longer pink and vegetables are tender, stirring after half the cooking time to break apart. Drain. Stir in sauerkraut, apple, brown sugar, vinegar, caraway seed and pepper; cover. Microwave at High 2 to 3 minutes, or until heated, stirring once during cooking.

Use to stuff one chicken or two Cornish game hens, or serve as four side dish servings.

If desired, wrap, label and freeze two side dish servings no longer than 2 weeks. To defrost and heat, microwave at 70% (Medium-High) 4 to 6½ minutes, stirring once during cooking.

Cabbage & Bratwurst ▲

1 fully cooked bratwurst, cut
    into ½-in. pieces
1 cup shredded cabbage,
    page 124
2 tablespoons shredded carrot
1 tablespoon apple juice or
    beer
⅛ teaspoon salt
⅛ teaspoon dry mustard
⅛ teaspoon celery seed
    Dash pepper

Serves 1

Combine all ingredients in
15-oz. individual casserole.
Microwave at High 2½ to 3½
minutes, or until cabbage is
tender and bratwurst is heated,
stirring after half the time.

Cabbage & Bratwurst for Two:
Double all ingredients. Prepare
as directed except use 1-qt.
casserole. Microwave at High 4
to 5 minutes.

Tacos

¼ lb. unseasoned bulk pork
    sausage
1 tablespoon chopped onion
½ teaspoon chili powder
⅛ teaspoon ground cumin
⅛ teaspoon garlic powder
    Dash dried crushed red
    peppers
1 tablespoon red salsa sauce
4 taco shells

Toppings:
1 mashed or sliced avocado
¼ cup dairy sour cream
1 cup shredded lettuce,
    page 124
¼ cup chopped green pepper
¼ cup chopped tomato
¼ cup shredded Cheddar
    cheese
1 tablespoon sliced pitted
    black olive

Serves 2

Crumble sausage into 22-oz. individual casserole. Stir in onion.
Cover with wax paper. Microwave at High 2 to 3½ minutes, or until
meat is no longer pink, stirring after half the time to break apart
meat. Drain.

Stir in chili powder, cumin, garlic powder, crushed red peppers
and salsa sauce. Cover with wax paper. Reduce power to 50%
(Medium). Microwave 3 to 4 minutes, or until flavors blend. Spoon
mixture into taco shells. Sprinkle with one or more of the toppings,
as desired.

Tacos for One: Wrap, label and freeze half of meat mixture no
longer than 2 weeks. To defrost and heat, microwave, covered with
wax paper, at 70% (Medium-High) 1 to 2 minutes. Prepare half the
amount of the topping ingredients.

Mostaccioli & Meat Sauce ▲

2 servings mostaccioli or
   elbow macaroni, page 133
⅓ lb. bulk hot Italian sausage
¼ cup chopped onion
1 clove garlic, minced
¼ cup sliced fresh mushrooms
   or 2 tablespoons sliced
   canned mushrooms, drained
1 can (8 oz.) whole tomatoes

2 tablespoons tomato paste
2 tablespoons chopped olives
½ teaspoon sugar
¼ teaspoon dried basil leaves
½ cup shredded mozzarella
   cheese
1 teaspoon grated Parmesan
   cheese

Serves 2

Microwave macaroni as directed. Set aside. Combine sausage, onion and garlic in 1-qt. casserole; cover. Microwave at High 3½ to 6 minutes, or until onion is tender, stirring once to break apart; drain. Stir in mushrooms, tomatoes, tomato paste, olives, sugar and basil. Cover. Microwave at High 2 to 4 minutes, or until mixture is heated and flavors blend, stirring once. Place macaroni on serving plate. Pour sauce over macaroni. Sprinkle with mozzarella, then Parmesan cheese. Reduce power to 50% (Medium). Microwave 4½ to 7 minutes, or until cheese melts and sauce is hot.

Mostaccioli & Meat Sauce for One: Prepare one serving macaroni; place in 6¾ × 4½-in. individual casserole. Prepare sauce as directed. Pour half of the sauce over macaroni. Sprinkle with half of the cheeses. Microwave at 50% (Medium) 2½ to 4½ minutes, or until cheese melts and sauce and macaroni are hot. Wrap, label and freeze remaining sauce no longer than 2 weeks. To defrost and heat one serving of frozen sauce, microwave, covered, at 70% (Medium-High) 3 to 5 minutes, stirring once during cooking. Continue with directions for one serving.

Wine-Braised Polish Sausage

½ small onion, thinly sliced
1 tablespoon red wine
1 fully cooked Polish sausage

Serves 1

In 15-oz. individual casserole combine onion and wine; cover. Microwave at High 30 to 60 seconds, or until onion is tender-crisp. Stir. Pierce sausage 2 or 3 times with fork. Place on onion; cover. Microwave at High 30 seconds to 1½ minutes, or until sausage is heated. Serve on rye bun topped with onions, if desired.

Wine-Braised Polish Sausages for Two: Double all ingredients. Prepare as directed except microwave onion and wine at High 1 to 2 minutes, and sausage at High 1½ to 2½ minutes.

Bacon-Wrapped Liver

¼ teaspoon instant beef
    bouillon granules
¼ cup hot water
1½ teaspoons packed brown
    sugar
⅛ teaspoon dry mustard
1 tablespoon white wine
1 teaspoon bouquet sauce
2 slices (¼ lb.) beef liver,
    ¼-in. thick
2 slices bacon
½ small onion, cut in half

Serves 1

Bacon-Wrapped Liver for Two:
Double all ingredients. Prepare
as directed except microwave
bacon at High 1½ to 2½ minutes and onion 1 to 2 minutes.
Reduce power to 50% (Medium).
Microwave liver 4 to 5 minutes.

How to Microwave Bacon-Wrapped Liver

Stir bouillon granules and hot
water in 2-cup measure until
granules dissolve. Stir in brown
sugar, mustard, wine and
bouquet sauce.

Place liver slices in 8 × 8-in.
baking dish. Pour brown sugar
marinade over liver. Let stand at
room temperature 1 hour or in
refrigerator 2 hours.

Place bacon in 1-qt. casserole.
Cover with paper towel. Microwave at High 1 to 1½ minutes,
or until light brown but not crisp.
Drain bacon on paper towel;
reserve drippings in casserole.

Secure onion quarters with
wooden picks. Place in casserole with reserved bacon drippings; cover. Microwave at High
1 to 1½ minutes, or until tender,
turning over and stirring to coat
after half the time.

Place one onion quarter in
center of each liver slice. Wrap
liver around onion. Wrap one
bacon slice around each roll;
secure with wooden pick. Place
rolls on roasting rack. Baste with
marinade. Cover with wax paper.

Reduce power to 50% (Medium). Microwave 1 to 2 minutes,
or until liver is no longer pink,
turning over and basting with
marinade after half the time. Do
not overcook.

Chicken Livers & Pasta ►

½ serving fettuccine,
    page 131
2 teaspoons butter or
    margarine, divided
1½ teaspoons grated Parmesan
    cheese
¼ small onion, thinly sliced
    and separated into rings
¼ cup sliced fresh mushrooms
1 tablespoon chopped green
    pepper
1 tablespoon snipped fresh
    parsley
⅛ teaspoon salt
⅛ teaspoon garlic powder,
    divided
    Dash pepper
½ small tomato, cut into thin
    wedges
¼ lb. chicken livers

Serves 1

Prepare fettuccine as directed. Place in 1-qt. casserole. Add 1 teaspoon butter and the Parmesan cheese; toss to melt butter and coat with cheese. Set aside. In 1-qt. casserole combine remaining 1 teaspoon butter, onion, mushrooms, green pepper, parsley, salt, dash of garlic powder and the pepper. Cover.

Microwave at High 1½ to 2½ minutes, or until vegetables are tender, stirring after half the time. Stir in tomato. Remove all vegetables; add to fettuccine. Add chicken livers and remaining dash of garlic powder to juice in casserole. Cover with wax paper. Reduce power to 50% (Medium). Microwave 1½ to 2 minutes, or just until livers are no longer pink, stirring once or twice. Spoon livers over fettuccine and vegetables.

Chicken Livers & Pasta for Two: Double all ingredients. Prepare as directed except microwave vegetables at High 2 to 3 minutes. Reduce power to 50% (Medium). Microwave livers 5½ to 6½ minutes.

Chicken Livers in Savory Mushroom Sauce

1½ teaspoons butter or
    margarine
¼ cup sliced fresh
    mushrooms
½ small onion, thinly sliced
    and separated into rings
¼ cup hot water
1 tablespoon vermouth
¼ teaspoon Worcestershire
    sauce

1½ teaspoons all-purpose flour
½ teaspoon instant beef
    bouillon granules
⅛ teaspoon dried oregano
    leaves
⅛ teaspoon dried basil leaves
    Dash salt
    Dash pepper
¼ lb. chicken livers

Serves 1

Place butter in 15-oz. individual casserole. Microwave at High 30 to 45 seconds, or until melted. Add mushrooms and onion. Microwave at High 45 to 60 seconds, or until vegetables are tender, stirring after half the time to coat with butter.

Stir hot water, vermouth, Worcestershire sauce, flour, bouillon granules, oregano, basil, salt and pepper into mushrooms and onion. Microwave at High 1 to 2½ minutes, or until thickened, stirring once. Stir in chicken livers. Cover with wax paper. Reduce power to 50% (Medium). Microwave 6 to 8 minutes, or until meat is no longer pink, stirring after half the time. (Centers will be slightly pink.) Let stand 5 minutes.

Chicken Livers in Savory Mushroom Sauce for Two: Double all ingredients. Prepare as directed except use 1-qt. casserole. Melt butter at High 30 to 45 seconds; microwave vegetables at High 1½ to 2½ minutes; thicken sauce at High 2½ to 3½ minutes. Reduce power to 50% (Medium). Microwave meat 8 to 10 minutes.

Poultry

General Poultry Tips

Economical poultry adapts to a variety of dishes. Microwaving not only saves time, but brings out its full flavor and juiciness. Poultry is a good choice for the small household. You can buy just enough chicken parts for one meal, create menu drama with Cornish hens, or microwave a whole chicken or small turkey to make enough meat for several meals.

Three to four ounces of cooked meat serves one. When buying bone-in poultry, allow ½ pound of chicken or ¾ pound of turkey per serving.

Fresh poultry should be wrapped loosely to allow air circulation and refrigerated no longer than 1 to 2 days. If you buy a whole bird, remove the giblets before storing. Wrap them separately and freeze, if desired. Never stuff poultry before refrigerating or freezing.

Cooked poultry will keep in the refrigerator 2 days. Remove any stuffing and refrigerate it separately. Poultry keeps up to 6 months in the freezer. Storage time for giblets is 3 months in the freezer.

Poultry Defrosting Chart

Type	Defrost Time at 50% (Medium)	Procedure
Chicken Whole	3 - 5½ min./lb.	Unwrap chicken; place breast side down in baking dish. Microwave for half the time. Turn breast side up. Microwave for remaining time. Loosen giblets. Place chicken in cold water until giblets can be removed and cavity is no longer icy.
Breasts Legs, thighs, wings	4 - 8 min./lb. 2½ - 5 min./lb.	Place package in oven. Defrost for half the time. Turn over. Defrost for one-fourth the total time. Unwrap package and separate pieces. Defrost remaining time. Let stand 5 minutes.
Turkey Whole	3½ - 5½ min./lb.	Unwrap turkey; place breast side down in baking dish. Microwave for one-fourth the time. Shield warm areas with foil, then turn turkey breast side up. Microwave for another one-fourth the time. Check for warm or brown spots, shielding them. Shield legs and wing tips. Turn turkey over. Rotate dish. Microwave for another one-fourth the time. Turn turkey over and microwave remaining time. Spread wings and legs from body; loosen giblets. Place turkey in cold water. Let stand 20 to 30 minutes, or until giblets and neck can be removed, and cavity is cool but not icy. Make sure breast is defrosted in areas under wings.
Cornish Hens	5 - 7 min./lb.	Unwrap hens; place breast side down in baking dish. Microwave for half the time. Turn breast side up. Microwave for remaining time. Loosen giblets. Place in cold water until giblets can be removed and cavity is no longer icy.

Making the Most of a Broiler-Fryer Chicken

One broiler-fryer chicken can be divided to make many meals. The chicken is microwaved, cut up and stored in ready-to-use packages. As a bonus, the rich broth is frozen in cubes for use in many recipes. On pages 88 and 89, you'll find recipes for cooked chicken. You may also substitute chicken for the turkey in the recipes on pages 92 to 95.

Stewed Chicken & Broth

3 lb. quartered broiler-fryer chicken
1 cup hot water
1 medium carrot, cut length-wise in half, then into 3-in. pieces
1 celery stalk, cut into 3-in. pieces

1 small onion, thinly sliced and separated into rings
1 bay leaf
3 whole peppercorns
½ teaspoon salt

Makes 3 cups cut-up cooked chicken and 1¾ cups broth

How to Microwave Stewed Chicken & Broth

Arrange chicken pieces in 3-qt. casserole, bone side up and meaty portions to outside of casserole. Add remaining ingredients; cover.

Microwave at High 15 to 20 minutes, or until meat near bone is no longer pink; turn over and rearrange after half the time. Let stand, covered, 5 minutes. Remove chicken pieces; set aside to cool.

Skim fat from broth. Strain and pour into 14-cube ice tray. Freeze. Remove chicken from bone. Cut into pieces. Wrap, label and freeze in quantities of ½ cup.

How to Defrost Chicken Pieces & Broth Cubes

Chicken. Freeze chicken no longer than 4 weeks. To defrost ½ cup chicken pieces, microwave at 50% (Medium) 1 to 2 minutes, turning over after half the time. Let stand to complete defrosting.

Broth. Store frozen cubes in plastic bag no longer than 4 weeks. Defrost in small bowl as directed in chart, right.

Defrosting Broth Chart

One broth cube is about 2 tablespoons.		
No. of Cubes	Microwave Time at High	Broth Yield
2	1-2 min.	¼ cup
3	1½ - 2 min.	⅓ cup
4	1½ - 2½ min.	½ cup
8	3 - 4 min.	1 cup

Wine-Braised Chicken

　1 slice bacon, cut into ½-in.
　　pieces
　1 frozen broth cube,
　　defrosted, page 83*
1½ teaspoons all-purpose flour
　2 tablespoons white wine
　2 tablespoons shredded
　　carrot
　2 teaspoons snipped fresh
　　parsley
　⅛ teaspoon dried bouquet
　　garni seasoning
　　Dash pepper
　1 chicken breast half, ½ lb.
　½ small onion, thinly sliced
　　and separated into rings
　½ cup sliced fresh mush-
　　rooms or 1 can (2½ oz.)
　　sliced mushrooms, drained

Serves 1

Place bacon in 1-qt. square casserole. Microwave at High 30 to 60 seconds, or until brown. Drain fat, reserving 1 tablespoon. Combine broth and reserved fat in 2-cup measure. Stir in flour until smooth. Add white wine, carrot, parsley, bouquet garni and pepper.

Remove skin from chicken. Place meaty side down in casserole. Pour sauce over. Place onion rings on top; cover with wax paper. Reduce power to 50% (Medium). Microwave 9 to 11 minutes, or until meat near bone is no longer pink, turning over after half the time. Add mushrooms during last 2 minutes of cooking.

Wine-Braised Chicken for Two: Double all ingredients. Prepare as directed except use 8 × 8-in. baking dish. Microwave bacon at High 1½ to 2 minutes. Reserve 2 tablespoons fat. Reduce power to 50% (Medium). Microwave chicken with sauce 10 to 14 minutes, stirring in mushrooms during last 3 minutes.

*Or use ⅛ teaspoon instant chicken bouillon granules dissolved in 2 tablespoons hot water.

Tarragon Chicken ▲

　¼ cup diced carrot
　¼ cup thinly sliced celery
1½ teaspoons butter or
　　margarine
　1 chicken breast half, ½ lb.
　2 teaspoons all-purpose flour
　2 frozen broth cubes,
　　defrosted, page 83*

　¼ teaspoon dried tarragon
　　leaves
　¼ teaspoon onion powder
　¼ teaspoon bouquet sauce
1½ teaspoons dry sherry
　1 tablespoon dairy sour
　　cream, optional

Serves 1

Place carrot, celery and butter in 14-oz. oval individual casserole; cover. Microwave at High 1 to 2 minutes, or until vegetables are tender, stirring once. Place chicken, meaty side down, on vegetables. Mix remaining ingredients except sour cream. Pour over chicken. Cover loosely with plastic wrap. Microwave at High 3½ to 4 minutes, or until meat near bone is no longer pink, stirring sauce and turning breast over after half the time. Remove chicken to serving plate. Blend sour cream into sauce; spoon over chicken.

Tarragon Chicken for Two: Double all ingredients. Prepare as directed except use 1-qt. square casserole. Microwave vegetables and butter at High 2 to 3 minutes; chicken and sauce at High 5 to 7½ minutes.

*Or use ¼ teaspoon instant chicken bouillon granules dissolved in ¼ cup hot water.

Stuffed Drumsticks ▲

½ cup sliced fresh
    mushrooms, divided
1 tablespoon shredded
    mozzarella cheese
1½ teaspoons grated Parmesan
    cheese
1½ teaspoons unseasoned
    bread crumbs
2½ teaspoons olive oil, divided
  ½ teaspoon dried basil leaves

⅛ teaspoon dried oregano
    leaves
⅛ teaspoon onion powder
⅛ teaspoon salt
2 chicken drumsticks, ¼ lb.
    each
¼ cup tomato juice
1 tablespoon catsup
¼ teaspoon sugar
  Dash pepper

Serves 1

Chop enough mushrooms to equal 1 tablespoon. In small bowl mix chopped mushrooms, mozzarella, Parmesan, bread crumbs, 1½ teaspoons olive oil, basil, oregano, onion powder and salt.

With fingers, gently separate skin from meat on one side of each drumstick as far down leg as possible. Divide bread crumb stuffing evenly (about 1½ tablespoons for each) and push between meat and skin with spoon. Secure with wooden pick.

Arrange drumsticks in 6½ × 4-in. loaf dish, meaty portion to outside. Cover with wax paper. Microwave at High 4 to 5 minutes, or until meat is no longer pink on the outside. Drain fat. Set aside.

Measure tomato juice in 1-cup measure. Stir in catsup, remaining 1 teaspoon olive oil, sugar and pepper. Sprinkle remaining sliced mushrooms over chicken. Pour sauce over chicken. Cover with wax paper. Microwave at High 2 to 3 minutes, or until meat near bone is no longer pink and juices run clear, spooning sauce over chicken after half the time. Let stand 3 to 5 minutes.

Stuffed Drumsticks for Two: Double all ingredients. Prepare as directed except arrange drumsticks in 1-qt. square casserole. Microwave at High 5 to 7 minutes. Microwave sauce, mushrooms and drumsticks at High 3 to 5 minutes.

Marinated Chicken Wings

¼ cup soy sauce
2 tablespoons apricot
    preserves
1 tablespoon lemon juice
¼ teaspoon ground ginger
¼ teaspoon dry mustard
4 chicken wings, tips removed

Serves 1

In 2-cup measure mix soy sauce, apricot preserves, lemon juice, ginger and mustard. Microwave at High 45 to 60 seconds, or until warm and preserves are melted, stirring to dissolve after half the time.

Place chicken wings in plastic bag. Pour soy marinade over wings; close bag. Let stand 1 hour at room temperature or in refrigerator 2 hours. Remove wings; discard marinade. Arrange wings in 1-qt. square casserole. Cover with wax paper. Microwave at High 4 to 5 minutes, or until meat near bone is no longer pink, rearranging and turning over after half the time. Garnish with lemon slices, if desired.

Marinated Chicken Wings for Two: Double all ingredients. Prepare as directed except microwave marinade at High 1 to 1½ minutes. Place chicken wings in 2-qt. square casserole; cover. Microwave at High 7 to 8½ minutes.

Chicken Kiev

> 1 tablespoon plus 1½ teaspoons softened butter, divided
> ⅛ teaspoon snipped chives
> Dash garlic powder
> Dash white pepper
> 1 boneless chicken breast half, ½ lb.

Crumb Coating:

> 2 tablespoons corn flake crumbs
> 1½ teaspoons grated Parmesan cheese
> ¼ teaspoon dried parsley flakes
> ¼ teaspoon paprika

Serves 1

Chicken Kiev for Two: Double all ingredients. Prepare as directed except soften 2 tablespoons butter at 10% (Low) 20 to 40 seconds. Increase power to High. Melt 3 teaspoons butter 30 to 45 seconds. Microwave chicken 2½ to 4 minutes, rotating and rearranging chicken after half the time.

How to Microwave Chicken Kiev

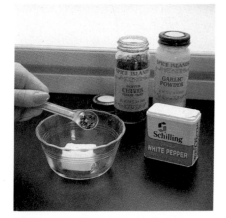

Place 1 tablespoon butter in small custard cup. Microwave at 10% (Low) 15 to 20 seconds, or until soft. Stir in chives, garlic powder and white pepper.

Shape the butter mixture into 1½ × 1-in. rectangle on small square of wax paper. Freeze 10 minutes, or until firm.

Pound chicken breast with flat side of meat mallet to ⅛-in. thickness. Set aside. Place remaining 1½ teaspoons butter in small bowl. Increase power to High. Microwave 15 to 30 seconds, or until melted. Set aside.

Luau Chicken

1 whole boneless chicken
   breast, 1 lb., cut in half
⅛ lb. ground veal
⅛ lb. ground pork
2 tablespoons finely chopped
   walnuts
1 tablespoon uncooked instant
   rice
1 tablespoon minced onion

1 tablespoon soy sauce
¼ teaspoon ground ginger
⅛ teaspoon ground nutmeg
1 tablespoon dark rum
1 tablespoon honey
1 tablespoon soy sauce
1 can (8 oz.) sliced pineapple,
   drained
2 teaspoons sesame seed

Serves 2

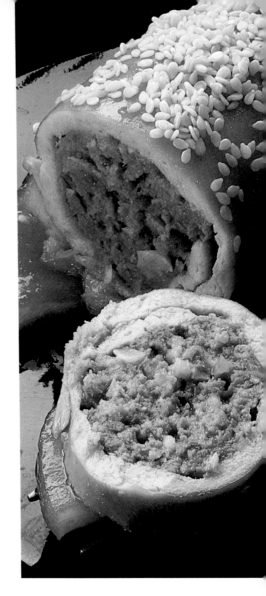

Pound chicken breast with flat side of meat mallet or edge of saucer to ¼-in. thickness. Mix ground veal, ground pork, walnuts, rice, onion, soy sauce, ginger and nutmeg. Spoon half on each chicken breast half. Roll breast around stuffing, tucking in ends and securing with wooden picks.

Mix rum, honey and soy sauce. Coat chicken rolls with some of the sauce. Set remaining sauce aside. Place each chicken roll in 14-oz. square individual casserole. Cover with wax paper. Microwave at High 5 minutes, rearranging casseroles after half the time. Drain.

Place two pineapple slices under each roll. Pour remaining sauce over each roll; sprinkle each with 1 teaspoon sesame seed. Microwave at High 1 to 3½ minutes, or until internal temperature is 170°F., rotating and rearranging dishes and chicken after half the time. Let stand 2 to 3 minutes.

Combine corn flake crumbs, Parmesan cheese, parsley flakes and paprika in shallow dish or on sheet of wax paper. Set aside.

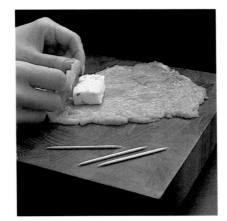

Place frozen butter rectangle at end of pounded chicken breast. Fold end over butter. Fold in sides, then continue rolling. Secure seam with wooden pick.

Roll in melted butter, then in crumbs. Place seam side down in 14-oz. square individual casserole. Microwave at High 1½ to 3 minutes, or until no longer pink and juices run clear, rotating dish ½ turn after half the cooking time.

Chicken Avocado Salad

1 medium avocado
1 teaspoon lime or lemon juice
½ cup cut-up cooked chicken,
    page 83
½ cup chopped tomato
2 tablespoons chopped green
    chilies
2 tablespoons chopped onion
¼ teaspoon salt
⅛ teaspoon ground cumin
    Dash cayenne pepper
½ cup shredded Cheddar
    cheese, divided

Serves 2

Cut avocado lengthwise around the pit into halves; twist to separate halves. Remove pit. Cut centers from shells; cut into ½-in. cubes; toss with lime juice. Place shells in 14-oz. oval individual casserole. Set aside.

In 1-qt. casserole mix chicken, tomato, green chilies, onion, salt, cumin and cayenne; cover. Microwave at High 2½ to 4 minutes, or until mixture is heated and onion is tender-crisp, stirring once during cooking. Stir in avocado cubes and 6 tablespoons cheese.

Place half of chicken mixture in each reserved avocado shell. Top with remaining 2 tablespoons cheese. Reduce power to 50% (Medium). Microwave 2½ to 3½ minutes, or until cheese melts. Serve shells topped with dairy sour cream, if desired.

Chicken Avocado Salad for One: Prepare as directed. Brush extra filled avocado shell with lime or lemon juice. Wrap in aluminum foil. Refrigerate no longer than 1 day. To reheat, microwave at 50% (Medium) 3½ to 5½ minutes.

Pineapple Chicken in Lettuce Leaves ▲

2 large lettuce leaves,
    page 124
½ can (8 oz.) crushed
    pineapple, drained
2 tablespoons chopped green
    pepper
2 teaspoons chopped green
    onion
⅛ teaspoon five spice powder
½ cup cut-up cooked chicken,
    page 83
2 teaspoons sunflower nuts
1 teaspoon sweet and sour
    sauce

Serves 1

Remove lettuce leaves from head as directed. Place lettuce leaves on plate. Microwave 30 seconds to 1½ minutes, or until slightly softened. Cool.

Combine pineapple, green pepper, green onion, and five spice powder in 1-qt. casserole. Microwave at High 1½ to 2½ minutes, or until green pepper is tender. Stir in chicken, sunflower nuts and sweet and sour sauce. Spoon half onto center of each lettuce leaf; fold lettuce around filling. Secure with wooden picks. Place in 1-qt. casserole or 14-oz. oval individual casserole; cover. Microwave at High 1 to 2 minutes, or until heated. Serve over hot cooked rice, page 133, with additional sweet and sour sauce, if desired.

Pineapple Chicken in Lettuce Leaves for Two: Double all ingredients. Prepare as directed except microwave lettuce at High 45 seconds to 2 minutes; vegetables 2½ to 4 minutes; wrapped chicken 1½ to 2½ minutes.

Chicken Chop Suey ▶

1 tablespoon soy sauce
2 teaspoons cornstarch
1 teaspoon sugar
⅛ teaspoon ground ginger
½ cup cut-up cooked chicken,
    page 83
¼ medium green pepper, cut
    into ⅛-in. strips
¼ cup thinly sliced celery
1 green onion, thinly sliced
2 frozen broth cubes,
    defrosted, page 83*
¼ cup sliced fresh mushrooms
½ teaspoon bottled oriental
    brown gravy sauce
1 tablespoon salted cashews,
    optional

Serves 1

In medium bowl mix soy sauce, cornstarch, sugar and ginger. Add chicken, tossing to coat. Set aside. Combine green pepper, celery, green onion and broth in 1-qt. square casserole; cover. Microwave at High 1½ to 2½ minutes, or until celery and green pepper are tender.

Stir in chicken mixture, mushrooms and gravy sauce; cover. Microwave at High 1½ to 2 minutes, or until mixture is heated and mushrooms are tender, stirring after half the cooking time. Serve over hot cooked rice, page 133, if desired. Sprinkle with cashews.

Chicken Chop Suey for Two:
Double all ingredients. Prepare as directed except use 2-qt. casserole. Microwave vegetables in broth at High 2½ to 3 minutes. Add chicken, mushrooms and gravy. Microwave at High 3 to 4 minutes.

*Or use ¼ teaspoon instant chicken bouillon granules dissolved in ¼ cup hot water.

Mulligatawny Stew

⅓ cup chopped onion
1 tablespoon butter or
    margarine
1 tablespoon all-purpose flour
1 can (16 oz.) whole tomatoes,
    drained
½ cup cut-up cooked chicken,
    page 83
4 frozen broth cubes,
    defrosted, page 83*

1 small apple, peeled and
    chopped
4 whole cloves
4 whole peppercorns
1 teaspoon curry powder
    Dash ground cinnamon
½ cup half and half

Serves 2

Combine onion and butter in 2-qt. casserole; cover. Microwave at High 4 to 5 minutes, or until tender, stirring after half the cooking time. Mix in flour. Stir in tomatoes, chicken, broth, apple, cloves, peppercorns, curry powder and cinnamon. Microwave, uncovered, at High 10 to 15 minutes, or until thickened, stirring 2 or 3 times during cooking. Remove cloves and peppercorns.

Gradually add half and half to stew mixture, stirring constantly. Serve immediately.

Mulligatawny Stew for One: Refrigerate one serving no longer than 2 days. To reheat, microwave at 70% (Medium-High) 2½ to 3½ minutes, stirring after half the time.

*Or use ½ teaspoon instant chicken bouillon granules dissolved in ½ cup hot water.

Making the Most of Turkey

How to Microwave & Carve 6-lb. Turkey

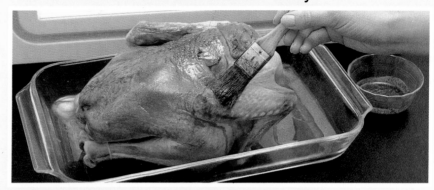

Turkey needn't be a once-a-year occasion for the small household, with leftovers that go on forever. Treat yourself to a small turkey or turkey roast. Carve what you want for the first meal, slice some for cold sandwiches, and cube the rest to freeze for a few of the delicious main dishes on the following pages.

Tie legs together. Place turkey, breast side down, in 12 × 8-in. baking dish. Microwave at High 10 minutes. If desired, baste with a mixture of 1 tablespoon melted butter and 1 tablespoon bouquet sauce. Rotate ½ turn. Reduce power to 50% (Medium). Microwave 30 minutes. Turn turkey breast side up; rotate ½ turn. Baste.

Microwave at 50% (Medium) 40 to 60 minutes, or until thermometer in meatiest part of thigh registers 185°F., rotating 2 or 3 times. Legs should move freely and juices run clear. Let stand, tented with foil, 20 to 30 minutes.

To carve, hold drumstick and pull away from body; cut between thigh and body to leg joint. Pull leg out and back, using point of knife to disjoint it. Cut thigh off drumstick at joint.

Slice thigh and drumstick meat parallel to bone, turning for even slices. Make a long horizontal cut above wing joint into body frame. Disjoint wing from body.

Cut thin, even slices down to horizontal cut, beginning halfway up the breast. Continue to slice white meat. Carve one side at a time.

Cut turkey into ½-in. cubes, if desired, for use in the following recipes. The yield is about 5 cups cut-up turkey. Wrap, label and freeze in quantities of ½ cup. To defrost, microwave one package at a time at 50% (Medium) 1 to 2 minutes, turning over after half the time. Let stand to complete defrosting.

How to Microwave 2-lb. Frozen Turkey Roast

Set aside gravy packet. Transfer roast from foil pan to 9 × 5-in. loaf dish. Cover with wax paper. Microwave at High 5 minutes. Rotate ¼ turn. Reduce power to 50% (Medium). Microwave 15 to 35 minutes, or until internal temperature reaches 175°F., rotating 2 or 3 times. Let stand 5 minutes.

Prepare gravy, if desired. Remove roast from dish. Use ¼ cup less water than called for in conventional directions. Add gravy mix and water to drippings. Microwave at High 6 to 8 minutes, or until thickened, stirring every 2 minutes.

Cut turkey into ½-in. pieces, if desired. The yield is about 3 cups cut-up turkey. Wrap, label and freeze in quantities of ½ cup. To defrost, microwave one package at a time at 50% (Medium) 1 to 2 minutes, turning over after half the time. Let stand to complete defrosting.

Turkey Broccoli Layer

½ cup frozen chopped broccoli
1 tablespoon chopped onion
2 teaspoons butter or
   margarine, divided
1 teaspoon all-purpose flour
¼ teaspoon prepared mustard
⅛ teaspoon salt

Dash pepper
¼ cup milk
1 tablespoon shredded Swiss
   cheese
1 slice bread, toasted
½ cup cut-up cooked white
   turkey meat, opposite

Serves 1

Place broccoli in small bowl. Cover with plastic wrap. Microwave at High 1 to 2 minutes, or until tender, stirring after half the time. Drain. Set aside. Place onion and 1 teaspoon butter in 2-cup measure. Cover with plastic wrap. Microwave at High 1½ to 2½ minutes, or until tender, stirring after half the time. Stir in flour, mustard, salt and pepper. Blend in milk.

Microwave at High 30 to 60 seconds, or until thickened, stirring after half the time. Stir in cheese. Trim crust from toast. Crumble crust pieces into custard cup. Microwave remaining 1 teaspoon butter at High 15 to 30 seconds, or until melted. Stir into crumbs, tossing to coat. Place trimmed toast on serving plate. Layer with broccoli, turkey and sauce. Sprinkle crumbs on top. Reduce power to 50% (Medium). Microwave 2 to 3 minutes, or until heated.

Turkey Broccoli Layer for Two: Double all ingredients. Prepare as directed except microwave broccoli at High 1½ to 2½ minutes; onion and butter, 2 to 3 minutes; sauce 1 to 1½ minutes; and butter 30 to 45 seconds. Reduce power to 50% (Medium). Microwave 3½ to 5 minutes.

Turkey Pot Pie ▲

Pastry:
¼ cup all-purpose flour
¼ teaspoon salt
1 tablespoon plus 1½
    teaspoons shortening
1 to 2 tablespoons ice water
1 or 2 drops yellow food
    coloring

Filling:
1 new potato, peeled and cut
    into ½-in. cubes
¼ cup diced carrot

2 tablespoons chopped onion
4 frozen broth cubes,
    defrosted, page 83*
2 teaspoons all-purpose flour
½ teaspoon dried parsley
    flakes
⅛ teaspoon salt
    Dash poultry seasoning
    Dash pepper
½ cup cut-up cooked turkey,
    page 90

Serves 1

To prepare pastry, combine flour and salt in small bowl. Cut in shortening until particles resemble small peas. In custard cup or small bowl combine water and food coloring. Sprinkle flour mixture with 1 teaspoon water at a time while tossing with a fork, until particles cling together and can be shaped into a ball. Wrap in plastic wrap and refrigerate. Mix all filling ingredients except turkey in 15-oz. individual casserole. Cover with wax paper. Microwave at High 5 to 7 minutes, or until vegetables are fork tender, stirring every 2 minutes. Stir in turkey. Set aside.

Roll pastry on lightly floured pastry cloth. Using an inverted 10-oz. custard cup as a guide, cut a circle 4½ inches in diameter. Prick surface with fork. Transfer pastry to wax paper. Sprinkle with paprika, if desired. Microwave at High 45 seconds to 1½ minutes, or until pastry appears dry, rotating after half the time. Remove from wax paper and place on top of filling in casserole.

Turkey Pot Pies for Two: Double all ingredients. Prepare as directed except use two 15-oz. individual casseroles. Microwave pastry at High 3 to 4 minutes, rotating after half the time.

*Or use ½ teaspoon instant chicken bouillon granules dissolved in ½ cup hot water.

Turkey Paprika ►

½ cup cut-up cooked white
    turkey meat, page 90
2 tablespoons chopped onion
1 teaspoon olive oil
1½ teaspoons butter or
    margarine
1½ teaspoons all-purpose flour
1 frozen broth cube,
    defrosted, page 83*
2 tablespoons half and half
¾ teaspoon paprika
    Hot cooked rice or Rice
    Ring, page 132

Serves 1

In 14-oz. square casserole combine turkey, chopped onion and olive oil; cover. Microwave at High 1½ to 2½ minutes, or until onion is tender and turkey is hot. Set aside.

Place butter in 1-cup measure. Microwave at High 20 to 30 seconds, or until melted. Stir in flour. Blend chicken broth, half and half, and paprika into butter and flour. Microwave at High 45 seconds to 1½ minutes, or until thickened, stirring once during cooking. Pour sauce over turkey. Reduce power to 50% (Medium). Microwave, uncovered, 1½ to 2½ minutes, or until very hot. Serve with rice or Rice Ring.

Turkey Paprika for Two:
Double all ingredients. Prepare as directed except use 1-qt. casserole for turkey and 2-cup measure for sauce. Microwave turkey mixture at High 2½ to 3½ minutes. Melt butter 30 to 45 seconds. Thicken sauce 1 to 1½ minutes. Reduce power to 50% (Medium). Microwave meat and sauce 2 to 3 minutes.

*Or use ⅛ teaspoon instant chicken bouillon granules dissolved in 2 tablespoons hot water.

Turkey & Stuffing Casserole ►

1 tablespoon plus 1½
   teaspoons butter or
   margarine, divided
2 tablespoons sliced fresh
   mushrooms
1½ teaspoons all-purpose flour
⅛ teaspoon salt
   Dash pepper
¼ cup milk
1 drop bouquet sauce

½ cup cut-up cooked white
   turkey meat, page 90
1 tablespoon chopped celery
1 tablespoon chopped onion
1 teaspoon dried parsley
   flakes
   Dash ground sage
2 frozen broth cubes,
   defrosted, page 83*
¾ cup unseasoned bread
   cubes

Serves 1

Place 1½ teaspoons butter and the mushrooms in 14-oz. square individual casserole. Microwave at High 45 seconds to 1½ minutes, or until butter melts and mushrooms are tender. Stir in flour, salt and pepper. Blend in milk. Microwave at High 45 seconds to 1½ minutes, or until thickened, stirring every 30 seconds. Stir in bouquet sauce and turkey. Set aside.

In 2-cup measure combine remaining 1 tablespoon butter, the celery, onion, parsley flakes, sage and broth; cover. Microwave at High 1 to 2 minutes, or until vegetables are tender, stirring after half the time. Add bread cubes, tossing to coat. Let stand, covered, 1 to 3 minutes to absorb moisture. Arrange stuffing on top of turkey and gravy in casserole. Microwave at High 1 to 2 minutes, or until heated.

Turkey & Stuffing Casseroles for Two: Double all ingredients. Prepare as directed except microwave mushrooms and butter in 2-cup measure at High 1 to 2 minutes. Thicken sauce at High 1½ to 3 minutes. Add turkey. Divide between two 14-oz. square individual casseroles. Microwave vegetables and butter at High 2 to 3 minutes. Microwave turkey and stuffing at High 1 to 3 minutes.

*Or use ¼ teaspoon instant chicken bouillon granules dissolved in ¼ cup hot water.

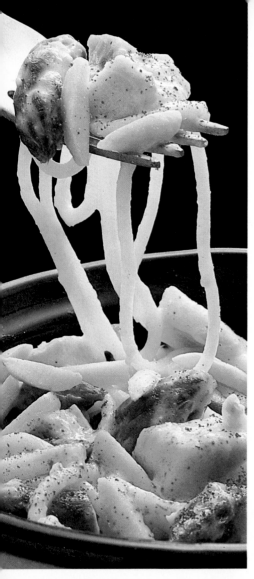

Turkey Asparagus Parmesan

½ serving spaghetti, page 131
2 tablespoons grated
  Parmesan cheese
1 tablespoon half and half or
  milk
½ cup frozen asparagus cuts
1 tablespoon butter or
  margarine
1 tablespoon all-purpose flour

¼ teaspoon salt
⅛ teaspoon dried thyme leaves
3 frozen broth cubes,
  defrosted, page 83*
2 tablespoons white wine
½ cup cut-up cooked turkey,
  page 90
1 tablespoon slivered almonds
  Paprika

Serves 1

Prepare spaghetti as directed. Place in 15-oz. individual casserole. Toss with Parmesan cheese and half and half. Set aside. Place frozen asparagus in small bowl; cover with wax paper. Microwave at High 1 to 2 minutes, or until heated and tender, stirring after half the time. Drain. Set aside.

Place butter in 2-cup measure. Microwave at High 30 to 45 seconds, or until melted. Stir in flour, salt and thyme. Blend broth and wine into butter and flour mixture. Microwave at High 1 to 2 minutes, or until thickened, stirring after half the time.

Stir turkey and asparagus into sauce. Mix with spaghetti. Top with slivered almonds; sprinkle with paprika. Microwave at High 1½ to 3 minutes, or until heated, rotating and rearranging dish after half the time.

Turkey Asparagus Parmesan for Two: Double all ingredients. Prepare as directed except use two 15-oz. individual casseroles, and 4-cup measure for sauce. Melt butter at High 30 to 45 seconds; microwave asparagus 2 to 3 minutes; thicken sauce 2 to 4 minutes; microwave all 3½ to 4½ minutes.

*Or use ½ teaspoon instant chicken bouillon granules dissolved in ¼ cup plus 2 tablespoons hot water.

Turkey Spaghetti

1 serving spaghetti, page 131
1 green onion, chopped
1 teaspoon butter or margarine
1 tablespoon all-purpose flour
⅛ teaspoon dried oregano
  leaves
⅛ teaspoon dried basil leaves
  Dash garlic powder
  Dash pepper

1 bay leaf
½ cup milk
2 frozen broth cubes,
  defrosted, page 83*
1 tablespoon sliced pimiento
½ cup cut-up cooked turkey,
  page 90
  Grated Parmesan or Romano
  cheese

Serves 1

Prepare spaghetti as directed. In 1-qt. casserole combine onion and butter; cover. Microwave at High 1 to 2 minutes, or until tender. Mix in flour, oregano, basil, garlic powder, pepper and bay leaf. Stir in milk, broth, pimiento and turkey. Microwave, uncovered, at High 3½ to 5 minutes, or until thickened, stirring twice during cooking. Serve over spaghetti. Sprinkle with cheese.

Turkey Spaghetti for Two: Double all ingredients except bay leaf. Microwave onion and butter at High 1½ to 2½ minutes. Thicken sauce at High 7 to 9 minutes.

*Or use ¼ teaspoon instant chicken bouillon granules dissolved in ¼ cup hot water.

Turkey & Wild Rice Casserole

1 serving wild rice, page 133
½ cup sliced fresh mush-
     rooms or 1 can (2½ oz.)
     sliced mushrooms, drained
¼ cup chopped celery
2 tablespoons chopped onion
1½ teaspoons butter or
     margarine
⅛ teaspoon dried basil leaves
⅛ teaspoon salt
     Dash pepper
     Dash garlic powder
1½ teaspoons all-purpose flour
¼ teaspoon instant chicken
     bouillon granules
¼ cup half and half
½ cup cut-up cooked turkey,
     page 90
1 tablespoon slivered
     almonds
1 slice (1 oz.) Provolone or
     mozzarella cheese, cut
     diagonally into quarters

Serves 1

Prepare rice as directed. Set
aside. Combine mushrooms,
celery, onion, butter, basil, salt,
pepper and garlic powder in
15-oz. individual casserole.
Cover. Microwave at High 2 to 3
minutes, or until tender, stirring
after half the time. Stir in flour.
Blend in bouillon granules and
half and half. Microwave,
uncovered, at High 1½ to 3
minutes, or until slightly
thickened, stirring twice during
cooking. Stir in wild rice, turkey
and almonds. Top with cheese
pieces. Reduce power to 50%
(Medium). Microwave 2½ to 4
minutes, or until mixture is
heated and cheese melts,
rotating after half the time.

**Turkey & Wild Rice Casserole
for Two:** Double all ingredients.
Prepare as directed except
microwave vegetables at High 4
to 5 minutes. Thicken sauce at
High 2 to 4 minutes. Reduce
power to 50% (Medium). Microwave casserole 6½ to 9 minutes.

Hot Turkey & Olive Salad ▲

½ cup cut-up cooked turkey,
     page 90
¼ cup finely diced celery
2 tablespoons chopped
     pecans
2 tablespoons chopped
     pimiento-stuffed olives
1 tablespoon mayonnaise or
     salad dressing
1 teaspoon lemon juice

⅛ teaspoon salt
¼ teaspoon dried parsley
     flakes
1½ teaspoons butter or
     margarine
1 teaspoon all-purpose flour
⅛ teaspoon dry mustard
¼ cup half and half
1 medium tomato

Serves 1

In 1-qt. bowl combine turkey, celery, pecans, olives, mayonnaise,
lemon juice, salt and parsley flakes. Set aside. Place butter in
2-cup measure. Microwave at High 30 to 45 seconds, or until
melted. Stir in flour and dry mustard. Blend in half and half.

Reduce power to 50% (Medium). Microwave sauce 1 to 2½
minutes, or until thickened, stirring every 30 seconds. Stir into
turkey mixture. Slice tomato into eighths to within ¼ inch of base.
Spread sections out to form a cup. Fill cup with turkey salad.

Hot Turkey & Olive Salad for Two: Double all ingredients.
Prepare as directed except microwave sauce 3 to 4 minutes.

Cornish Hen Veronique ▲

1 tablespoon plus 1 teaspoon
   butter or margarine, divided
1 teaspoon bouquet sauce
1 Cornish game hen, 1½ to 1¾
   lbs., defrosted, page 82
2 teaspoons all-purpose flour
1 frozen broth cube, defrosted,
   page 83*

2 tablespoons white wine
⅛ teaspoon grated lemon peel
½ cup fresh seedless green
   grapes, halved
1 tablespoon whipping cream
   or milk
1 serving rice, page 133

Serves 1

Place 1 teaspoon butter in small dish. Microwave at High 15 to 30 seconds, or until melted. Blend in bouquet sauce. Tie drumsticks of hen together with heavy string. Place hen, breast side down, on roasting rack. Brush with half of the bouquet-butter mixture. Microwave at High 8 to 12 minutes, or until juices run clear and meat near bone is no longer pink, rotating ½ turn every 2 to 3 minutes. Turn hen breast side up after half the cooking time and baste with remaining bouquet sauce. Let stand, covered, while preparing sauce and rice.

Place remaining 1 tablespoon butter in 2-cup measure. Microwave at High 30 to 45 seconds, or until melted. Blend in flour, broth, wine and lemon peel. Microwave at High 30 to 45 seconds, or until thickened, stirring every 15 seconds. Stir in grapes and cream. Prepare rice as directed. Place hen on rice. Pour sauce over top.

Cornish Hens Veronique for Two: Double all ingredients. Prepare as directed except microwave hens 16 to 20 minutes.

*Or use ⅛ teaspoon instant chicken bouillon granules dissolved in 2 tablespoons hot water.

Cranberry-Apple Glazed Cornish Hen

1 Cornish game hen, 1½ to 1¾
   lbs., defrosted, page 82
¼ teaspoon salt
⅛ teaspoon pepper
1 small apple, cut into ½-in.
   pieces
1 tablespoon packed brown
   sugar

Glaze:
½ cup whole berry cranberry
   sauce
1 teaspoon cognac or brandy
¼ teaspoon ground cinnamon

Serves 1

Wash hen and pat dry. Sprinkle cavity with salt and pepper. Toss apple pieces with brown sugar. Place apple pieces in hen cavity. Tie drumsticks together with heavy string. Place hen, breast side down, on roasting rack. In small bowl mix cranberry sauce, cognac and cinnamon. Baste hen with half the cranberry glaze.

Microwave at High 8 to 12 minutes, or until juices run clear and meat near bone is no longer pink, rotating ½ turn every 2 to 3 minutes. Turn hen breast side up after half the cooking time and baste with remaining glaze.

Variation:
Honey-Soy Glazed Cornish Hen: Substitute half small onion, quartered, for the apple and brown sugar in cavity. Substitute 2 tablespoons honey, 1 tablespoon soy sauce, ¼ teaspoon dry mustard and ⅛ teaspoon ground ginger for the glaze ingredients. Microwave glaze at High 30 to 45 seconds, or until heated, stirring to dissolve honey. Continue as directed.

Glazed Cornish Hens for Two: Double all ingredients. Prepare as directed except microwave hens at High 16 to 20 minutes.

96

Split Cornish Hen With Savory Stuffing

1 Cornish game hen, 1½ to 1¾ lbs., defrosted, page 82
1 teaspoon butter or margarine
1 teaspoon bouquet sauce
2 slices bacon
1 tablespoon chopped onion
½ cup seasoned stuffing mix
3 tablespoons hot water
2 teaspoons slivered almonds
⅛ teaspoon dried marjoram leaves
Dash pepper

Serves 2

Cut hen along backbone with a sharp knife. Turn over; cut breast in half. Place butter in small dish. Microwave at High 10 to 15 seconds, or until melted. Stir in bouquet sauce. Brush hen halves with mixture. Set aside.

Place bacon between paper towels. Microwave at High 1½ to 2 minutes, or until brown; crumble. Place onion in small bowl; cover with wax paper. Microwave at High 20 to 30 seconds, or until tender. Mix in bacon, stuffing mix, hot water, almonds, marjoram and pepper. Mound the stuffing mixture in center of 8 × 8-in. baking dish. Arrange the hen halves on top of stuffing, meaty side up. Cover with wax paper. Microwave at High 8 to 10 minutes, or until juices run clear and meat near bone is no longer pink, rotating ½ turn every 2 or 3 minutes. Let stand, covered, 5 minutes.

Split Cornish Hen With Savory Stuffing for One: Prepare as directed above. Wrap, label and freeze one hen half and stuffing no longer than 4 weeks. To defrost and heat, place in 1-qt. casserole. Cover with wax paper. Microwave at 50% (Medium) 7 to 10 minutes, or until very hot, rotating twice and turning over after half the time.

Cornish Hen With Lettuce Stuffing ▲

¼ cup hot water
¼ cup uncooked instant rice
1 tablespoon butter or margarine
1 large orange
⅓ cup chopped lettuce, page 124
1 tablespoon chopped walnuts
¼ teaspoon salt
¼ teaspoon onion powder
⅛ teaspoon ground allspice, divided
1 Cornish game hen, 1½ to 1¾ lbs., defrosted, page 82
1½ teaspoons cornstarch
1 teaspoon packed brown sugar
1 tablespoon sherry
¼ teaspoon bouquet sauce

Serves 1

Place water in 2-cup measure. Cover with plastic wrap. Microwave at High 1 minute, or until boiling. Stir in rice. Cover and set aside. Place butter in small dish. Microwave at High 30 to 45 seconds, or until melted.

Grate ⅛ teaspoon orange peel. Set aside. Cut orange in half. Squeeze juice from one half (about ¼ cup). Set aside for glaze mixture. Peel remaining half, removing seeds and membrane. Chop segments into small pieces. Stir orange segments, orange peel, lettuce, walnuts, salt, onion powder, dash allspice and the melted butter into rice. Stuff hen with rice mixture. Secure cavity with wooden picks. Place hen, breast side down, on roasting rack. Set aside.

In 1-cup measure combine reserved orange juice, cornstarch, brown sugar, sherry, bouquet sauce and remaining dash of allspice. Stir well. Microwave at High 45 seconds to 1½ minutes, or until thickened, stirring once.

Brush hen with half the glaze mixture. Cover with wax paper. Microwave at High 8 to 12 minutes, or until juices run clear and meat near bone is no longer pink, rotating ½ turn every 2 to 3 minutes. Turn hen breast side up after half the cooking time and baste with remaining glaze. Let stand, covered, 5 minutes.

Cornish Hens With Lettuce Stuffing for Two: Double all ingredients. Prepare as directed except thicken glaze 1½ to 2 minutes; microwave hens 16 to 20 minutes.

Fish & Seafood

Many markets offer fish at the meat counter, so you can buy just the amount you need. In the frozen food case, you'll find individually frozen whole trout, fish steaks and lobster tails. Three to four ounces of cooked boneless fish makes one serving. To store, remove fish from packaging, wrap loosely in foil or plastic and use within 24 hours. If you wish to freeze fish, check with the butcher to make sure it has not been previously frozen.

◄ Lobster Thermidor

1 frozen lobster tail, 14 to 16 oz.
2 tablespoons water
1 tablespoon lemon juice
2 tablespoons butter or margarine
1 teaspoon snipped fresh chives
1 tablespoon all-purpose flour
1 teaspoon instant chicken bouillon granules
Dash white pepper
½ cup half and half
1 egg yolk, slightly beaten
1 tablespoon dry sherry
¼ cup shredded Cheddar cheese
Paprika

Serves 2

Place frozen lobster tail in 10 × 6-in. baking dish. Cover with plastic wrap. Microwave at 50% (Medium) 5 to 7 minutes, or until exterior is warm and center remains slightly frozen, turning over every 2 minutes. Let stand, covered, 5 minutes to complete defrosting. Using kitchen scissors or a sharp knife, cut away thin underside of lobster shell to expose meat. Place tail, meat side up, in 10 × 6-in. baking dish. Combine water and lemon juice. Pour over tail; cover with plastic wrap.

Microwave at 50% (Medium) 5 to 8 minutes, or until meat is opaque, rotating ¼ turn every 2 minutes and shielding exposed meat with a small piece of foil, if necessary. Let stand, covered, 5 minutes. Remove meat from shell. Cut into small pieces. Rinse shell, cutting away any remaining membrane. Drain and set aside.

Place butter and chives in 2-cup measure. Increase power to High. Microwave 30 to 60 seconds, or until butter melts. Stir in flour, bouillon granules and white pepper. Blend in half and half. Microwave at High 1 to 2½ minutes, or until thickened, stirring every 30 seconds. Stir a small amount of hot mixture into beaten egg yolk. Return to hot mixture, stirring constantly. Mix in sherry. Microwave at High 30 to 60 seconds, or until heated. Stir. Add meat.

Place reserved shell in 14-oz. oval individual casserole. Spoon meat and sauce into shell. Sprinkle with cheese and paprika. Reduce power to 50% (Medium). Microwave 4½ to 6½ minutes, or until cheese melts and meat mixture is heated. Serve in two patty shells and garnish with parsley sprigs, if desired.

Scalloped Oysters

2 slices bacon
1 can (8 oz.) oysters, drained, 2 tablespoons liquid reserved
⅓ cup crushed saltine crackers
¼ cup half and half
2 tablespoons finely chopped celery
¼ teaspoon dry mustard
Dash pepper
2 tablespoons butter or margarine

Serves 1

Place bacon on roasting rack or between paper towels. Microwave at High 1½ to 2 minutes, or until brown. Crumble and set aside. Place oysters and reserved liquid in 15-oz. individual casserole. Sprinkle with crushed crackers. Pour half and half over crackers. Sprinkle with celery, then dry mustard and pepper.

Place butter in small dish. Microwave at High 30 to 45 seconds, or until melted. Pour over crackers. Top with crumbled bacon. Reduce power to 50% (Medium). Microwave 6 to 8 minutes, or until mixture is slightly set and heated.

Scalloped Oysters for Two:
Double all ingredients. Prepare as directed except use two 15-oz. individual casseroles. Microwave bacon at High 3½ to 4 minutes, butter 45 to 60 seconds. Reduce power to 50% (Medium). Microwave final mixture 8 to 11 minutes.

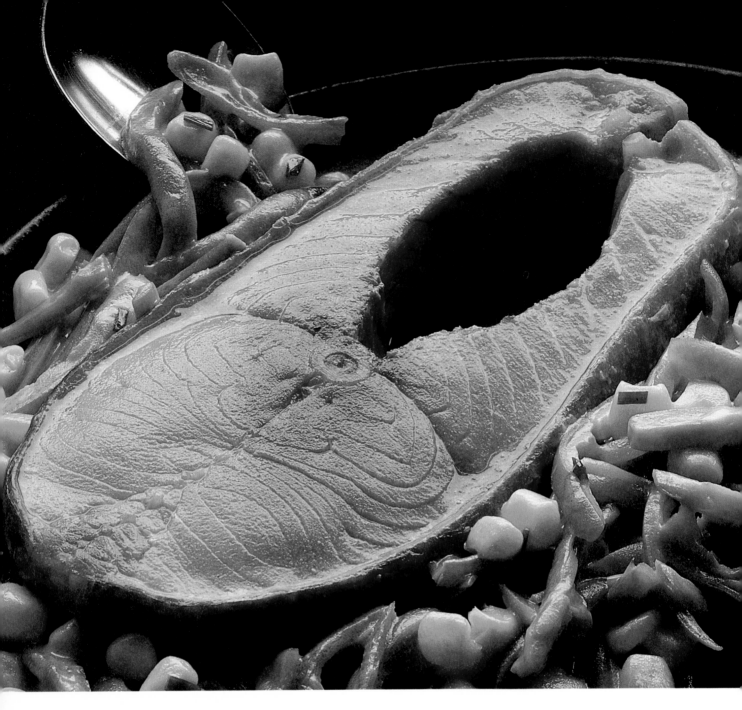

Fish Storage & Defrosting Chart

Type of Fish	Maximum Refrigerator Time	Maximum Freezer Time	Defrost Time at 50% (Medium)*
Whole Fish	1 day	2 months	3 - 5 minutes/lb.
Salmon & Halibut Steaks	1 day	2 months	10 - 13 minutes/lb.
Fillets	1 day	2 to 3 months	3 - 5 minutes/lb.
Lobster Tail	1 day	2 to 3 months	4½ - 8½ minutes/lb.
Scallops	1 day	2 to 3 months	3 - 5½ minutes/lb.
Shrimp, colossal	1 day	2 to 3 months	3 - 5½ minutes/lb.

*Defrost fish in original package. Microwave at 50% (Medium) as directed in chart, turning over or stirring after half the time. Rinse under cold water until no longer icy.

◄ Salmon Steak With Succotash

1 salmon steak, about ½ lb.
1 teaspoon lemon juice
1 teaspoon butter or margarine
1 teaspoon all-purpose flour
½ teaspoon dried chives
¼ teaspoon salt
    Dash pepper
½ cup frozen French-style
    green beans
¼ cup frozen whole-kernel corn
2 tablespoons half and half

Serves 1

Place salmon steak in 14-oz. square individual casserole. Sprinkle lemon juice over salmon. Cover loosely with plastic wrap. Microwave at 50% (Medium) 2 to 3 minutes, or until fish flakes easily, turning over after half the time. Drain juices. Cover tightly with plastic wrap and let stand.

Place butter in 2-cup measure. Increase power to High. Microwave 10 to 20 seconds, or until melted. Stir in flour, chives, salt and pepper. Mix in green beans, corn and half and half. Reduce power to 50% (Medium). Microwave 2½ to 3½ minutes, or until sauce thickens and vegetables are tender and hot, stirring every minute. Arrange vegetables around salmon and serve.

Salmon Steaks With Succotash for Two: Double all ingredients. Prepare as directed except use two 14-oz. square individual casseroles. Divide ingredients between casseroles. Microwave at 50% (Medium) 3½ to 5 minutes. Increase power to High. Microwave butter in 4-cup measure 20 to 30 seconds. Add remaining ingredients to melted butter. Reduce power to 50% (Medium). Microwave vegetables and sauce 4 to 6 minutes.

Broccoli-Stuffed Trout ►

1 frozen whole trout, 6 oz.
½ cup frozen chopped broccoli
2 green onions, chopped
1 tablespoon butter or
    margarine
1 tablespoon chopped
    almonds
¼ teaspoon salt
¼ teaspoon lemon pepper
½ teaspoon lemon juice

Serves 1

Place frozen trout in shallow dish. Microwave at 50% (Medium) 1 to 1½ minutes, or until defrosted, turning over once during cooking time. Cavity will remain icy. Rinse in cold water until no longer icy. Pat dry with paper towel. Place broccoli in small dish. Increase power to High. Microwave 30 to 60 seconds, or until defrosted. Stir. Set aside.

Place onions and butter in small dish. Microwave at High 1 to 1½ minutes, or until tender. Mix in almonds, salt and lemon pepper. Place trout in 10 × 6-in. baking dish. Spoon three-fourths of broccoli mixture into trout cavity. Arrange remaining broccoli mixture around trout. Sprinkle trout with lemon juice. Cover with wax paper. Microwave at High 2 to 4 minutes, or until fish flakes easily.

Broccoli-Stuffed Trout for Two: Double all ingredients. Prepare as directed except defrost two trout at 50% (Medium) 1½ to 2 minutes. Increase power to High. Microwave broccoli 45 seconds to 1½ minutes, butter and onion 1½ to 2 minutes and stuffed fish 4 to 6 minutes.

Spinach-Stuffed Sole

1 sole fillet, ½ lb.
1 pkg. (10 oz.) frozen chopped
  spinach, divided
⅓ pkg. (3 oz.) cream cheese
2 tablespoons herb-seasoned
  stuffing mix
1 tablespoon chopped pecans
1 teaspoon milk
1 teaspoon mayonnaise or
  salad dressing
⅛ teaspoon salt
  Paprika

Serves 2

Variation:

Crab-Stuffed Sole: Prepare as
directed except substitute
one-half can (6½ oz.) crab meat
for chopped spinach.

Stuffed Sole for One: Prepare
as directed except microwave
only one half fillet at 50%
(Medium) 3 to 5 minutes.

Wrap, label and freeze the other
half fillet no longer than 2
weeks. To defrost and cook,
microwave at 50% (Medium) 9
to 12 minutes, or until fish flakes
easily and stuffing is heated.

How to Microwave Spinach-Stuffed Sole

Divide fillet into four pieces,
cutting parallel to head end. Cut
diagonal slits in two pieces to
within ¼ inch of corner. Place
cut piece on top of uncut piece.
Place in 1-qt. square casserole.
Set aside.

Place spinach package in oven.
Microwave at High 3 to 4
minutes, or until defrosted,
turning over after half the time.
Let stand to complete defrosting. Place in strainer and press
out moisture.

Place cream cheese in medium
bowl. Microwave at High 15 to
30 seconds, or until soft. Stir in
stuffing mix, pecans, milk,
mayonnaise, salt and ⅓ cup of
the spinach.

Coquilles St. Jacques

¼ lb. fresh bay scallops
¼ cup sliced fresh mushrooms
1 green onion, chopped
1 tablespoon butter or margarine, divided
1 tablespoon white wine
½ teaspoon lemon juice
2 teaspoons all-purpose flour
⅛ teaspoon salt
⅛ teaspoon dried savory leaves
Dash white pepper
1 tablespoon milk
2 tablespoons shredded Swiss cheese
2 teaspoons dry bread crumbs
1 teaspoon snipped fresh parsley

Serves 1

In 1-qt. casserole combine scallops, mushrooms, green onion, 1½ teaspoons butter, wine and lemon juice; cover. Microwave at 50% (Medium) 3 to 4 minutes, or until scallops flake easily and are opaque, stirring after half the time.

Remove scallops and vegetables to 10-oz. custard cup, reserving liquid in casserole. Stir flour, salt, savory and white pepper into liquid. Blend in milk. Increase power to High. Microwave 30 to 60 seconds, or until thickened, stirring after half the cooking time. Stir in cheese. Pour over scallops in custard cup, tossing to coat.

Place remaining 1½ teaspoons butter in small bowl. Microwave at High 15 to 30 seconds, or until melted. Stir in bread crumbs and parsley. Sprinkle over scallops. Reduce power to 50% (Medium). Microwave 1½ to 2½ minutes, or until heated.

Coquilles St. Jacques for Two: Double all ingredients. Prepare as directed except use two 10-oz. custard cups. Microwave scallops and vegetables at 50% (Medium) 5 to 7 minutes. Increase power to High. Microwave sauce 30 seconds to 2 minutes. Microwave butter 30 to 45 seconds. Reduce power to 50% (Medium). Microwave both cups 2½ to 4½ minutes, rotating twice during cooking.

Open slits on cut fish to form pockets. Stuff each fillet with half of the spinach mixture. Sprinkle with paprika. Cover with wax paper.

Reduce power to 50% (Medium). Microwave fillets 6 to 9 minutes, or until fish flakes and center is set, rotating dish every 3 minutes. Let stand 5 minutes.

Increase power to High. Microwave remaining spinach 1½ to 3 minutes, or until heated. Serve with fish.

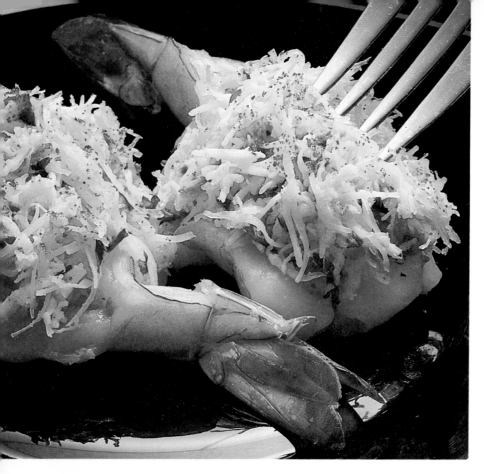

Stuffed Shrimp

¼ lb. fresh, raw colossal
   shrimp (4 shrimp)
½ fresh lemon, cut in half
 1 tablespoon butter or
   margarine
½ can (6½ oz.) crab meat,
   drained and cartilage
   removed
 1 tablespoon dry bread
   crumbs
 1 tablespoon snipped fresh
   parsley
   Dash salt
   Dash cayenne pepper
   Paprika

Serves 1

Stuffed Shrimp for Two:
Double all ingredients. Prepare
as directed except use two
6¾ × 4½-in. individual
casseroles. Microwave at 50%
(Medium) 5 to 7 minutes,
rearranging casseroles twice
during cooking.

How to Microwave Stuffed Shrimp

Clean shrimp by loosening shell from the leg side; peel off carefully, leaving tail intact. Make a cut down middle of back with a sharp knife from tail to thick end.

Do not cut all the way through. With point of knife, loosen and remove vein. To butterfly, flatten the cut thick end of the shrimp.

Place shrimp in 6¾ × 4½-in. individual casserole, tails toward center. Squeeze 1 teaspoon juice from one lemon wedge into small dish.

Place butter in medium bowl. Microwave at High 30 to 45 seconds, or until melted. Stir in crab, bread crumbs, parsley, lemon juice, salt and cayenne.

Divide stuffing into four equal parts; mound on shrimp. Sprinkle with paprika. Garnish with remaining lemon wedge, if desired. Cover with wax paper.

Reduce power to 50% (Medium). Microwave 3 to 5 minutes, or until shrimp are opaque, rotating after half the time. (Do not overcook, shrimp will curl.)

Cheesy Tuna

½ serving macaroni shells,
    page 131
2 tablespoons thinly sliced
    celery
1 tablespoon chopped onion
1 tablespoon chopped green
    pepper
1 tablespoon butter or
    margarine
2 teaspoons all-purpose flour
⅛ teaspoon salt
    Dash pepper
½ teaspoon Worcestershire
    sauce
⅓ cup milk
1 can (3¼ oz.) tuna, drained
¼ cup shredded Cheddar or
    American cheese
¼ cup crushed potato chips

Serves 1

Prepare macaroni shells as directed. Set aside. In 15-oz. individual casserole combine celery, onion, green pepper and butter; cover. Microwave at High 1½ to 2½ minutes, or until vegetables are tender, stirring after half the time.

Stir in flour, salt, pepper and Worcestershire sauce. Blend in milk. Microwave at High 1 to 2 minutes, or until thickened, stirring after half the time. Stir in macaroni shells, tuna and cheese. Sprinkle with crushed potato chips.

Reduce power to 50% (Medium). Microwave 2 to 4 minutes, or until heated, rotating casserole once during cooking.

Cheesy Tuna for Two: Double all ingredients. Prepare as directed except use 1-qt. casserole. Microwave vegetables at High 2 to 3 minutes and sauce at High 2 to 4 minutes. Reduce power to 50% (Medium). Microwave casserole 3 to 5 minutes, rotating twice during cooking.

Salmon Croquettes With Sour Cream Lemon Sauce ▲

½ cup hot water
1 tablespoon butter or
    margarine
⅔ cup instant mashed potato
    mix
1 tablespoon chopped onion
1 tablespoon chopped celery
1 can (3¾ oz.) red salmon,
    cleaned and drained
1 tablespoon snipped fresh
    parsley
½ teaspoon salt

¼ teaspoon dry mustard
⅛ teaspoon pepper
1 egg, separated
½ teaspoon lemon juice
¼ teaspoon Worcestershire
    sauce
2 tablespoons corn flake
    crumbs
¼ teaspoon paprika
1 tablespoon lemon juice
½ teaspoon sugar
¼ cup dairy sour cream

Serves 2

Place water and butter in 2-cup measure. Microwave at High 1½ to 2 minutes, or until boiling. Stir in potato mix with fork. Set aside. Place onion and celery in small bowl; cover. Microwave at High 30 to 60 seconds, or until tender. Mix in potatoes, salmon, parsley, salt, mustard, pepper, egg white, lemon juice and Worcestershire sauce. Divide into four equal portions, shaping each into 3-in. patty.

In small shallow dish or on wax paper mix crumbs and paprika. Coat salmon patties with crumbs; place on roasting rack. Cover with wax paper. Microwave at High 3 to 4 minutes, or until heated and firm to touch, rotating dish twice during cooking.

In small bowl beat egg yolk with fork or wire whip. Blend in lemon juice and sugar, then sour cream. Reduce power to 50% (Medium). Microwave, uncovered, 2 to 3 minutes, or until thickened, stirring every 30 seconds. Pour over salmon patties.

Eggs, Cheese & Milk

Egg and cheese dishes are good choices for the small household. They're quick and easy to make, and since eggs and cheese keep well in the refrigerator, they're convenient to keep on hand. Pre-shredded cheese not only simplifies preparation, but is available in smaller packages than block cheese. Wrap leftover cheese tightly to keep it fresh for future use. These egg recipes are based on large eggs, which measure about 3 tablespoons apiece.

◄ Crab Quiche

1 microwaved 7-in. pie shell, page 144
¼ cup chopped green pepper
1 small onion, thinly sliced
1 can (6½ oz.) crab meat, drained, rinsed and cartilage removed
½ cup shredded Cheddar cheese
3 eggs, slightly beaten
¼ cup milk
¼ teaspoon salt
⅛ teaspoon pepper

Serves 2

Prepare pie shell as directed. Place green pepper and onion in medium bowl; cover. Microwave at High 2 to 3 minutes, or until tender, stirring after half the time. Stir in remaining ingredients. Pour into pie shell. Place in oven on inverted saucer. Reduce power to 50% (Medium). Microwave quiche 11 to 16 minutes, or until center is slightly soft set. Let stand 5 minutes.

Crab Quiche for One:
Refrigerate one serving no longer than 2 days. To reheat, microwave at 50% (Medium) 2½ to 5 minutes.

Broccoli & Cauliflower Strata

½ cup chopped frozen cauliflower
½ cup frozen chopped broccoli
1 slice white bread
½ cup shredded Cheddar cheese, divided
1 egg, slightly beaten
2 tablespoons milk
1½ teaspoons chopped onion
⅛ teaspoon salt
Dash pepper

Serves 1

In small bowl combine cauliflower and broccoli. Cover with plastic wrap. Microwave at High 1 to 2 minutes, or until defrosted, stirring after half the time. Chop finely. Drain, pressing out moisture.

Place bread slice in 14-oz. square individual casserole. Sprinkle with ¼ cup of cheese, the chopped vegetables and remaining cheese. In small bowl combine egg, milk, chopped onion, salt and pepper. Pour over vegetables and cheese. Cover and refrigerate at least 4 hours.

To microwave, cover with wax paper. Reduce power to 50% (Medium). Microwave 8 to 12 minutes, or until set and liquid is no longer visible, rotating 3 or 4 times during cooking. Let stand, covered, 3 minutes.

Broccoli & Cauliflower Strata for Two: Double all ingredients. Prepare as directed except microwave vegetables at High 2½ to 3½ minutes. Use two 14-oz. square individual casseroles. Reduce power to 50% (Medium). Microwave casseroles 10 to 13 minutes.

Shrimp Egg Foo Yung ►

Patties:

2 tablespoons chopped green
   pepper
1 tablespoon chopped onion
1 small clove garlic, minced
2 teaspoons cornstarch
¾ cup frozen cooked shrimp,
   defrosted and chopped
½ cup fresh bean sprouts
2 eggs, slightly beaten
¼ teaspoon salt

Sauce:

2 teaspoons cornstarch
½ teaspoon sugar
½ teaspoon instant beef
   bouillon granules
2 teaspoons soy sauce
1 teaspoon white wine
½ cup hot water

Serves 2

In small bowl combine green pepper, onion and garlic. Cover with plastic wrap. Microwave at High 1½ to 3 minutes, or until tender, stirring once. Blend in cornstarch. Stir in shrimp, sprouts, eggs and salt.

Preheat browning dish at High 4 minutes. Using ½-cup measure pour two patties onto browning dish. Reduce power to 50% (Medium). Microwave 2 to 3 minutes, or until base is set and brown. Turn patties. Microwave at 50% (Medium) 1 to 2 minutes, or until set.

In 1-cup measure combine cornstarch, sugar and bouillon granules. Add soy sauce and white wine. Slowly stir in hot water until bouillon dissolves. Increase power to High. Microwave sauce 1 to 2½ minutes, or until clear and slightly thickened, stirring 2 or 3 times. Pour over patties.

Shrimp Egg Foo Yung for One: Refrigerate one serving no longer than 2 days. To reheat, place patty on serving plate; cover with wax paper. Microwave at 50% (Medium) 4 to 6 minutes, rotating and turning over after half the time.

Mock Eggs Benedict ▲

1 English muffin, split and
   toasted
2 slices Canadian bacon
4 tablespoons hot water,
   divided
½ teaspoon vinegar, divided
2 eggs

Sauce:

2 teaspoons butter or
   margarine
2 teaspoons all-purpose flour
⅛ teaspoon salt
   Dash pepper
⅓ cup milk
2 tablespoons shredded
   Monterey Jack cheese
½ teaspoon lemon juice

Serves 2

Top each muffin half with one slice bacon. In each of two 6-oz. custard cups combine 2 tablespoons water and ¼ teaspoon vinegar. Cover with plastic wrap. Microwave at High 30 to 60 seconds, or until boiling. Break one egg into each cup. Reduce power to 50% (Medium). Microwave eggs 1 to 1½ minutes, or until most of the egg white is opaque but not set, rotating cups every 45 seconds. Let stand 2 to 3 minutes, shaking cups gently once or twice during cooking.

Place butter in small bowl. Increase power to High. Microwave 30 to 45 seconds, or until melted. Stir in flour, salt and pepper until smooth. Blend in milk. Microwave at High 1½ to 2¼ minutes, or until thickened, stirring every minute. Stir in cheese and lemon juice until smooth. Place one egg on each muffin half. Top with sauce.

Egg Cooking Chart

Egg Type	Amount	Microwave Time	Procedure
Poached	1 2	¾-1½ min. 1-1½ min.	Place 2 tablespoons water and ¼ teaspoon vinegar in 6-oz. custard cup. Cover with plastic wrap. Microwave at High 30 to 60 seconds, or until boiling. Break eggs into cups. Cover with plastic wrap. Reduce power to 50% (Medium). Microwave until most of the egg white is opaque, but not set. Let stand, covered, 2 to 3 minutes. When poaching more than one egg, rotate cups every 45 seconds.
Fried	1 2	¾-1¼ min. 1-1½ min.	Preheat browning dish at High 3 minutes. Add 1 tablespoon butter. Tilt dish to coat. Crack eggs into dish. Cover. Microwave at High until set. Let stand, covered, 1 minute.
Scrambled	1 2	½-¾ min. 1¼-1¾ min.	Place 1 tablespoon butter in 12- or 14-oz. individual casserole. Microwave at High 30 to 45 seconds, or until melted. Add one egg and 1 tablespoon milk or two eggs and 2 tablespoons milk. Scramble with fork. Microwave at High, stirring to break apart after half the time. Eggs will appear moist after cooking. Let stand 1 to 4 minutes to complete cooking.

Yogurt ▶

⅓ cup non-fat dry milk powder
1 qt. whole milk
⅓ cup plain yogurt

Makes 4 cups

Place dry milk in 2-qt. casserole or bowl; slowly stir in whole milk until dry milk dissolves. Microwave at High 8 to 11 minutes, or until 190°F., stirring once or twice. Let mixture cool to 115°F. Stir a small amount of hot mixture into yogurt; return to milk mixture, stirring constantly. Cover with plastic wrap.

Insert microwave thermometer through plastic so it rests in center of the milk mixture. If using 2-qt. casserole, thermometer will not stand up in center; hold it as you check temperature in center periodically.

Reduce power to 30% (Medium-Low). When temperature falls below 115°F., microwave 30 seconds to 3½ minutes, or until 115°F. Allow mixture to stand in oven undisturbed 3 to 4 hours. Check temperature every 30 minutes. If temperature falls below 110°F., microwave at 30% (Medium-Low) 30 seconds to 1 minute, or until temperature reaches 115°F. Mixture will appear set. Transfer to refrigerator to chill. Refrigerate yogurt no longer than 2 weeks.

Flavor Variations:
Stir one or a combination of the following into 1 cup yogurt:

1 tablespoon jam or preserves
1 tablespoon maple or fruit-flavored syrup
½ cup fresh chopped or mashed fruit
2 tablespoons chopped dried fruit ▶

French Toast ▲

1½ teaspoons butter or margarine
1 egg
1 tablespoon half and half or milk
½ teaspoon powdered sugar
Dash ground cinnamon
Dash salt
2 slices French bread, 1-in. thick

Serves 1

Place butter in custard cup. Microwave at High 30 to 60 seconds, or until melted. In medium bowl beat egg, half and half, sugar, cinnamon and salt. Gradually beat in butter. Preheat browning dish at High 4 minutes. Meanwhile, soak bread in egg mixture. Arrange slices in dish, gently pressing down with spatula. Microwave at High 30 seconds. Turn and rearrange slices. Microwave 30 to 45 seconds, or until light brown and set. Serve with warm syrup, or sprinkle with powdered sugar, if desired.

French Toast for Two: Double all ingredients. Prepare as directed except microwave second side 30 to 60 seconds.

Mexican Egg Casserole

1 egg
½ teaspoon all-purpose flour
1½ teaspoons milk
½ cup shredded Cheddar cheese
½ cup shredded Monterey Jack cheese
3 tablespoons chopped green chilies
1 tablespoon chopped black olives
1½ teaspoons chopped onion
¼ teaspoon salt
⅛ teaspoon chili powder

Serves 1

In medium bowl beat egg. Mix in flour and milk. Stir in remaining ingredients. Pour into 14-oz. square individual casserole. Cover with wax paper. Microwave at 50% (Medium) 7 to 8 minutes, or until egg mixture is set, rotating every 3 minutes. Let stand 3 to 5 minutes.

Mexican Egg Casserole for Two: Double all ingredients. Prepare as directed except use two 14-oz. individual casseroles and 1 can (4 oz.) chopped green chilies. Microwave at 50% (Medium) 9 to 13 minutes.

Cheese-Filled Shells With Clam Sauce ▲

6 jumbo macaroni shells,
    page 131

Filling:
¾ cup ricotta cheese
½ cup shredded mozzarella
    cheese
¼ cup grated Parmesan
    cheese
1 egg, slightly beaten
¼ teaspoon garlic juice
½ teaspoon dried basil leaves
¼ teaspoon salt
    Dash pepper

Sauce:
1½ teaspoons cornstarch
½ cup tomato juice
¼ cup clam juice
2 teaspoons olive oil
¼ teaspoon garlic juice
¼ teaspoon dried basil leaves
¼ teaspoon sugar
⅛ teaspoon pepper
2 tablespoons milk
½ teaspoon red wine

Serves 2

Prepare macaroni shells as directed. In small bowl blend all filling ingredients; fill each shell with about 1½ tablespoons. Place seam side down in 1-qt. square casserole.

Place cornstarch in 2-cup measure. Add small amount tomato juice, stirring until smooth. Mix in remaining tomato juice, clam juice, olive oil, garlic juice, basil, sugar and pepper. Microwave at High 3 to 5 minutes, or until slightly thickened, stirring every minute. Blend in milk and wine. Pour over shells. Reduce power to 50% (Medium). Microwave 5 to 9 minutes, or until heated, rotating ¼ turn every 2 minutes. Let stand 3 minutes.

Cheese-Filled Shells With Clam Sauce for One: Wrap, label and freeze one serving in 12-oz. individual casserole. To defrost and heat, cover frozen casserole with wax paper. Microwave at 50% (Medium) 8 to 10 minutes, rotating ¼ turn every 2 minutes.

Rarebit

1 English muffin, split and
    toasted
¼ cup beer
1½ teaspoons butter or
    margarine
½ teaspoon Worcestershire
    sauce
⅛ teaspoon dry mustard
1 cup shredded Cheddar
    cheese
1½ teaspoons all-purpose flour

Serves 1

Place toasted muffin on serving plate. In 2-qt. casserole mix beer, butter, Worcestershire sauce and dry mustard. Microwave at High 2 minutes, or until mixture boils and butter melts. Shake cheese and flour in plastic bag until cheese is coated. Gradually stir cheese into beer mixture. Reduce power to 50% (Medium). Microwave 1 to 2 minutes, or until cheese melts and mixture is smooth, stirring vigorously with wire whip after each minute. Serve immediately over muffin.

Rarebit for Two: Double all ingredients. Prepare as directed except microwave beer mixture at High 2 to 3 minutes. Reduce power to 50% (Medium). Microwave 2 to 3 minutes.

Cheese Fondue ▶

1 cup shredded Swiss
   cheese
1½ teaspoons all-purpose flour
¼ cup plus 2 tablespoons
   white wine

½ teaspoon Kirsch
Dash pepper
Dash nutmeg
French bread, cut into
   cubes

Serves 1

Shake cheese and flour in plastic bag until cheese is coated.
Place wine in deep 2-qt. casserole. Microwave at 70% (Medium-
High) 1 to 2 minutes, or until wine just begins to bubble around
edge. Do not boil. Stir in cheese, Kirsch, pepper and nutmeg.

Reduce power to 50% (Medium). Microwave 2 to 4 minutes, or
until cheese melts and mixture is smooth, stirring vigorously after
every minute. Serve with cubed French bread. Reheat as needed
at 50% (Medium).

Cheese Fondue for Two: Double all ingredients. Prepare as
directed except microwave wine at 70% (Medium-High) 2 to 3
minutes. Reduce power to 50% (Medium). Microwave cheese-wine
mixture 2 to 3 minutes.

Macaroni & Cheese

½ cup elbow macaroni,
   page 131
1½ teaspoons butter or
   margarine
1 small green onion, chopped
1½ teaspoons all-purpose flour
⅛ teaspoon salt
   Dash pepper

⅓ cup milk
2 tablespoons shredded
   Monterey Jack cheese
1½ teaspoons grated Parmesan
   cheese
2 tablespoons shredded
   Cheddar cheese

Serves 1

Prepare macaroni as directed. Set aside. Place butter in 4-cup
measure. Microwave at High 30 to 45 seconds, or until melted. Stir
in onion, flour, salt and pepper until smooth. Add milk in three
parts, stirring to blend. Microwave at High 1 to 2 minutes, or until
thickened, stirring after 1 minute and then every 30 seconds. Stir
drained macaroni into thickened sauce.

In 12-oz. individual casserole layer half of the macaroni mixture,
the Monterey Jack cheese, Parmesan cheese, remaining macaroni
and the Cheddar cheese. Reduce power to 50% (Medium).
Microwave 2 to 2½ minutes, or until macaroni is heated and
cheese melts, rotating after half the time.

Macaroni & Cheese for Two: Double all ingredients. Prepare as
directed except microwave flour-milk mixture at High 2 to 3½
minutes. In each of two 12-oz. individual casseroles layer
one-fourth of the macaroni mixture, half of the Monterey Jack
cheese, half of the Parmesan cheese, the remaining macaroni and
half of the Cheddar cheese. Reduce power to 50% (Medium).
Microwave 3 to 4 minutes, or until macaroni is heated and cheese
melts, rotating and rearranging casseroles after half the time.

General Vegetable Tips

One-half cup of cooked vegetable makes a single serving. Whenever possible, buy fresh vegetables in the amount you need, using the Yield Chart as a guide. Moisture content and maturity directly affect cooking times. Fresh vegetables contain more natural moisture and microwave faster, with less water, than vegetables picked late in the season.

This section provides directions for using extra servings of large vegetables. Directions for loose-packing vegetables are on page 8. Store frozen vegetables no longer than 3 months.

Vegetable Yield & Storage Chart

Fresh Vegetable	Yield per pound	Maximum Refrig. Time (Fresh)	Maximum Freezer Time
Artichokes, whole	2 whole	2 to 3 days	Do not freeze
Asparagus, cuts	16 to 20 spears	1 to 2 days	1 to 3 months
Beans, Green, cuts	3 cups	1 week	1 to 3 months
Beets	2 cups	2 weeks	1 to 3 months
Broccoli	1½ to 2 cups	5 days	1 to 3 months
Cabbage	2½ to 3 cups	1 week	Do not freeze
Carrots	3 cups	2 weeks	1 to 3 months
Cauliflower	1½ cups	1 week	1 to 3 months
Celery	2 cups	1 week	Do not freeze
Corn, ears	2 ears	1 to 2 days	1 to 3 months
Lettuce	2½ to 3 cups	5 days	Do not freeze
Mushrooms	6 cups	2 to 3 days	1 to 3 months
Peas	1 cup	5 days	1 to 3 months
Potatoes, whole	2 cups	Whole, in cool, dry place: 3 weeks	Do not freeze
Spinach	2 cups	5 days	1 to 3 months
Squash, Summer	2 cups	Whole, in cool, dry place: 5 days	1 to 3 months
Winter	1½ to 2 cups	Whole, in cool, dry place: 3 to 6 months	Mashed: 1 to 3 months
Tomatoes	2 cups	1 week	Do not freeze

Frozen Vegetable Cooking Chart

Vegetable	Amount	Microwave Time at High	Procedure (Use covered casserole)
Pouch	6 to 9 oz. 10 oz.	3 - 6 min. 6 - 9 min.	Flex pouch. Cut large "X" in one side. Place cut side down in 1-qt. casserole. Stir before serving.
Box	6 to 9 oz. 10 oz.	3 - 6 min. 6 - 9 min.	1-qt. casserole. 2 tablespoons water. Stir once. Let stand 2 to 3 minutes.
Bag	½ cup 1 cup	1 - 2½ min. 2 - 4 min.	12-oz. casserole. 1 teaspoon water. Stir once. 15- or 22-oz. casserole. 2 teaspoons water. Stir once.

Fresh Vegetable Cooking Chart

Vegetable	Amount	Microwave Time at High	Procedure (Use covered casserole)
Artichoke, whole	1 artichoke 2 artichokes	4 - 5 min. 5½ - 8½ min.	See page 127.
Asparagus, cuts	½ cup 1 cup	1½ - 2½ min. 3 - 4 min.	12-oz. casserole. 1 tablespoon water. Stir once. 22-oz. casserole. 2 tablespoons water. Stir once.
Beans, Green, cuts	½ cup 1 cup	3 - 4 min. 5 - 6 min.	12-oz. casserole. 2 tablespoons water. Stir once. 1-qt. casserole. ¼ cup water. Stir twice.
Beets, whole	¼ lb. or ½ lb.	7 - 8 min.	1-qt. casserole. ¼ cup water. Let stand 5 minutes.
Broccoli, cuts	½ cup 1 cup	1½ - 2 min. 3 - 4 min.	12-oz. casserole. 1 teaspoon water. Stir once. 22-oz. casserole. 2 teaspoons water. Stir once.
Cabbage, shredded or chopped	½ cup 1 cup	4 - 6 min. 2½ - 3½ min.	15-oz. casserole. 1 tablespoon water. Stir once. 1-qt. casserole. 2 tablespoons water. Stir once.
Carrots, sliced	½ cup 1 cup	1½ - 2 min. 2 - 3 min.	12-oz. casserole. 1 tablespoon water. Stir once. 15-oz. casserole. 2 tablespoons water. Stir once.
Cauliflower, flowerets	½ cup 1 cup	1½ - 2½ min. 2½ - 3½ min.	12-oz. casserole. 1 teaspoon water. Stir once. 22-oz. casserole. 2 teaspoons water. Stir once.
Corn, ears	1 ear 2 ears	2 - 5 min. 4½ - 10 min.	Wrap in plastic wrap. Turn over and rearrange after half the time.
Mushrooms, halved	1 cup 2 cups	1 - 1½ min. 1½ - 2 min.	12-oz. casserole. 1 teaspoon butter. Stir once. 22-oz. casserole. 2 teaspoons butter. Stir once.
Peas	½ cup 1 cup	1½ - 2 min. 2 - 3 min.	12-oz. casserole. 2 teaspoons water. Stir once. 22-oz. casserole. 1 tablespoon water. Stir once.
Potatoes, whole	1 potato 2 potatoes	3 - 5 min. 5 - 7½ min.	Prick well-scrubbed potatoes. Place in oven on paper towel. Turn over and rearrange once. Wrap in foil. Let stand 5 to 10 minutes.
Spinach, chopped	2 cups 4 cups	2 - 3 min. 2 - 4 min.	22-oz. casserole. 1 teaspoon water. Stir once. 1-qt. casserole. 2 teaspoons water. Stir once.
Squash, Acorn (2 lbs.)	½ squash 1 squash	5 - 8 min. 8½ - 11½ min.	Cover with plastic wrap. Rotate once. Let stand 5 to 10 minutes.

Canned Vegetables: Drain 7- to 9-oz. can, reserving 1 tablespoon liquid. Microwave in 12-oz. covered casserole at High 1 to 2 minutes, stirring once. For 14- to 20-oz. can, reserve 2 tablespoons liquid; use 1-qt. covered casserole. Microwave at High 2 to 3 minutes, stirring once.

Making the Most of Acorn Squash

Acorn squash is a versatile vegetable. Cook and serve right in the shell or use the mashed pulp in soup or bread. One squash serves two people. If you're cooking for one, refrigerate leftover cooked squash no longer than 2 days, or freeze as directed below.

Recipes using mashed squash:
Acorn Squash Soup, below
Applesauce Squash, opposite
Fresh Squash Bread, opposite

How to Microwave & Freeze Acorn Squash

Cut 1-lb. acorn squash in half crosswise. Scoop out seeds and fibers. Wrap each half in plastic wrap. Microwave at High 5 to 7 minutes, or until fork tender, rearranging after half the cooking time. Let stand 5 minutes. Scoop out cooked pulp; mash. Yields 1 cup mashed squash.

Package ½-cup or 1-cup quantities tightly in freezer bags, containers or heat sealable pouches. Place piece of plastic wrap directly on top of squash. Seal and label. Freeze no longer than 3 months.

To serve or to use in the following recipes, unwrap and place in 1-qt. casserole. Microwave ½-cup at High 2 to 3 minutes, or 1-cup 3 to 4½ minutes, stirring to break apart after half the time.

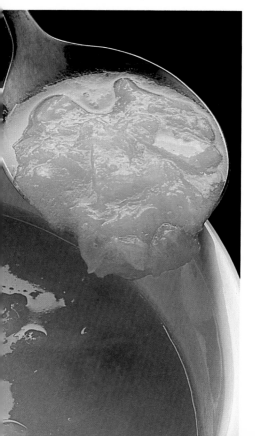

Acorn Squash Soup

1 tablespoon butter or
  margarine
1 tablespoon chopped onion
1 tablespoon grated carrot
½ cup mashed cooked acorn
  squash, above
½ cup hot water

½ teaspoon instant chicken
  bouillon granules
½ teaspoon packed brown
  sugar
⅛ teaspoon dry mustard
  Dash garlic powder
  Dash pepper

Serves 1

In 15-oz. individual casserole or bowl combine butter, onion and carrot; cover. Microwave at High 1 to 1½ minutes, or until vegetables are tender. Stir in remaining ingredients. Microwave, uncovered, at High 1½ to 2 minutes, or until heated.

Acorn Squash Soup for Two: Double all ingredients. Prepare as directed except use two 15-oz. casseroles. Microwave vegetables at High 1½ to 2 minutes; soup, 2 to 3 minutes.

Applesauce Squash

1 acorn squash, about 1 lb.,
   opposite

Filling:
2 tablespoons prepared
   applesauce
1 teaspoon honey
1 teaspoon butter or margarine
⅛ teaspoon salt
   Dash ground cinnamon
   Dash ground nutmeg

Serves 1

Microwave squash as directed.
Mash and freeze one squash
half as directed. Remove plastic
wrap from remaining squash
half. Mash cooked squash in
shell with fork.

In center of squash place
applesauce, honey, butter and
salt; mix. Sprinkle with cinnamon and nutmeg. Microwave,
uncovered, at High 1 to 1½
minutes, or until filling is heated.

Variations:
Brown Sugar Squash: Prepare
squash as directed, omitting
filling ingredients. Mix 1 tablespoon packed brown sugar, 1
tablespoon butter and ⅛ teaspoon salt into mashed squash
in shell. Sprinkle with 1
teaspoon chopped pecans.

Sour Cream Squash: Prepare
squash as directed, omitting
filling ingredients. Mix 1½
teaspoons butter or margarine
into mashed squash in shell.
Sprinkle with 1 teaspoon
slivered almonds and dash of
nutmeg. Top with 1 tablespoon
dairy sour cream before serving.

Squash for Two: Use both
halves of squash. Double
remaining ingredients, dividing
between each half. Prepare as
directed except microwave at
High 1½ to 2 minutes.

Fresh Squash Bread ▲

1 cup Dry Quick Bread Mix,
   page 135
2 tablespoons finely chopped
   walnuts
1 tablespoon sugar
⅛ teaspoon ground allspice
½ cup mashed cooked acorn
   squash, opposite
1 egg, slightly beaten

3 tablespoons orange juice
¾ teaspoon grated orange
   peel, divided
1 tablespoon butter or
   margarine
2 tablespoons graham cracker
   crumbs
1 tablespoon flaked coconut

Makes 1 loaf

Line bottom of 6½ × 4-in. loaf dish with wax paper. In medium bowl
mix quick bread mix, walnuts, sugar, allspice, squash, egg, orange
juice and ½ teaspoon orange peel just until combined. Spread in
prepared dish.

Place butter in 6-oz. custard cup. Microwave at High 30 to 45
seconds, or until melted. Mix in graham cracker crumbs, coconut
and remaining ¼ teaspoon orange peel. Set aside.

Reduce power to 50% (Medium). Microwave bread 3 minutes,
rotating once during cooking time. Sprinkle topping evenly on loaf,
pressing down lightly with fingers. Microwave at 50% (Medium) 2
to 6 minutes, or until top is light and springy to touch and no
uncooked batter remains on bottom and sides of dish, rotating dish
2 or 3 times. Let stand 5 minutes. Remove from loaf dish. Wrap
and refrigerate any leftover bread.

Making the Most of Broccoli & Cauliflower

A bunch of broccoli or a head of cauliflower yields from 3 to 6 servings. However, the fresh vegetable can be refrigerated for several days. Keep cauliflower in the original wrapper or cover loosely with plastic wrap. Store broccoli in plastic bag. Do not wash these vegetables until ready to use.

If you don't care to serve broccoli or cauliflower several days in a row, the extra servings can be blanched and frozen. For best quality, do this within 24 hours of purchase. Either fresh or frozen broccoli and cauliflower can be used in the recipes which follow. If you are using a frozen vegetable, do not defrost it first.

Recipes that use broccoli and cauliflower:
Broccoli Pizza Rounds, opposite
Broccoli Butter Toss, opposite
Broccoli-Cauliflower Pie,
   page 128
Cream of Broccoli Soup,
   page 128
Marinated Cauliflower Salad,
   page 129
Cauliflower With Cheese-
   Horseradish Sauce, page 129

How to Prepare & Freeze Broccoli & Cauliflower

Cut fresh broccoli and cauliflower into flowerets. Slice broccoli stems into 1-in. pieces. Blanch and freeze any unused portions.

Blanch by placing 1 cup broccoli or cauliflower cuts in 1½-qt. casserole with ½ cup water; cover. Microwave broccoli at High 1 to 2 minutes, or until vibrant green, and cauliflower at High 2 to 3 minutes, or until pliable but crisp, stirring after half the time. Drain.

Plunge hot vegetables immediately into ice water. Let stand in water to cool completely. Drain thoroughly.

Package ½-cup or 1-cup quantities tightly in freezer bags, containers or heat sealable pouches. Seal and label. Freeze no longer than 3 months.

To serve, microwave ½ cup at High 1 to 2½ minutes, and 1 cup at High 2 to 4 minutes. Do not cook vegetables for use in the following recipes.

120

Broccoli Pizza Rounds

2 teaspoons finely chopped
   onion
½ teaspoon olive oil
¼ cup chopped fresh tomato
1 tablespoon catsup
⅛ teaspoon ground oregano
⅛ teaspoon dried basil leaves
   Dash garlic salt
   Dash pepper
½ cup fresh or frozen broccoli
   cuts, opposite
2 teaspoons hot water
1 English muffin, split and
   toasted
¼ cup shredded mozzarella
   cheese
1 teaspoon grated Parmesan
   cheese

Serves 1

Place onion and olive oil in small bowl; cover. Microwave at High 1 to 1½ minutes, or until onion is tender, stirring once during cooking. Stir in tomato, catsup, oregano, basil, garlic salt and pepper. Microwave, uncovered, at High 1 to 1½ minutes, or until tomato is tender and spices are blended. Set aside.

Place broccoli and water in 15-oz. individual casserole or bowl. Microwave at High 1½ to 2 minutes, or until fork tender, stirring after half the time. Drain. Chop finely.

Arrange toasted muffin halves on plate. Spread 1 teaspoon tomato mixture on each. Divide broccoli equally between muffins. Pour remaining sauce over broccoli. Sprinkle mozzarella and Parmesan cheese over both halves. Microwave at High 1 to 2 minutes, or until cheese melts, rotating plate once.

Broccoli Pizza Rounds for Two: Double all ingredients. Prepare as directed except divide mixtures among four muffin halves. Microwave onion at High 1½ to 2 minutes; sauce, 2 to 2½ minutes; broccoli, 3 to 4 minutes; muffins, 1 to 2 minutes.

Broccoli Butter Toss ▲

½ cup fresh or frozen broccoli
   cuts or cauliflowerets,
   opposite
1 medium carrot, cut into
   2 × ¼-in. strips
2 teaspoons water

1½ teaspoons butter or
   margarine
1½ teaspoons snipped fresh
   parsley
   Dash salt
   Dash pepper

Serves 1

Place broccoli, carrot strips and water in small bowl or casserole; cover. Microwave at High 1 to 3 minutes, or until tender-crisp, stirring after half the time. Drain.

In 6-oz. custard cup combine butter, parsley, salt and pepper. Microwave at High 20 to 30 seconds, or until butter melts. Pour over broccoli and carrots, tossing to coat.

Variations:
Vegetables Almondine: Omit parsley and salt. Stir 1½ teaspoons slivered almonds and dash of garlic salt into butter.

Lemony Vegetables: Omit parsley. Stir 1 teaspoon sliced pimiento, ¼ teaspoon lemon juice and dash of dried basil leaves into butter.

Broccoli Butter Toss for Two: Double all ingredients. Prepare as directed except microwave vegetables at High 2 to 4 minutes and butter mixture, 30 to 45 seconds.

Broccoli-Cauliflower Pie ▲

Pastry:
⅓ cup all-purpose flour
⅓ cup whole wheat flour
2 tablespoons finely chopped
   pecans
¼ teaspoon salt
¼ cup plus 2 teaspoons
   shortening
2 to 4 tablespoons ice water

Filling:
1 cup fresh or frozen broccoli
   cuts, page 120
1 cup fresh or frozen
   cauliflowerets, page 120

1 tablespoon butter or
   margarine
1 tablespoon plus 1 teaspoon
   all-purpose flour
½ teaspoon coriander
¼ teaspoon salt
⅛ teaspoon pepper
½ cup milk
¼ cup shredded Swiss cheese,
   divided
¼ cup shredded Cheddar
   cheese, divided
1 tablespoon finely chopped
   pecans

Serves 2

Prepare and microwave pastry as directed for One Crust Pastry Shell, page 144, using ingredients listed above and adding chopped pecans with flours. Set aside.

For filling, place broccoli and cauliflower in 1-qt. square casserole; cover. Microwave at High 3 to 4 minutes, or until tender-crisp, stirring after half the time. Drain. Cover and set aside. Place butter in 2-cup measure. Microwave at High 30 to 45 seconds, or until melted. Stir in flour and seasonings. Gradually blend in milk.

Microwave at High 1½ to 3 minutes, or until thickened, stirring every 30 seconds. Pour over vegetables, tossing to coat. Stir in Swiss and Cheddar cheese, reserving 1 tablespoon of each for topping. Spread evenly in prepared pie shell. Sprinkle with reserved cheese and the pecans. Reduce power to 50% (Medium). Microwave 3 to 5 minutes, or until heated, rotating after half the time. Cover with wax paper and let stand 5 minutes.

Broccoli-Cauliflower Pie for One: Refrigerate one serving no longer than 2 days. To reheat, microwave at 50% (Medium) 2½ to 5 minutes, rotating after half the time.

Cream of Broccoli Soup

½ cup fresh or frozen broccoli
   cuts, page 120
2 teaspoons hot water
1 tablespoon butter or
   margarine
1 tablespoon all-purpose flour
½ teaspoon instant chicken
   bouillon granules
¼ teaspoon grated lemon peel
⅛ teaspoon dried chives
⅛ teaspoon onion powder
⅛ teaspoon salt
   Dash white pepper
¾ cup milk
   Croutons

Serves 1

Place broccoli and water in 15-oz. individual casserole or bowl. Microwave at High 1½ to 2 minutes, or until tender-crisp, stirring after half the time. Drain. Chop finely; return to casserole. Cover and set aside.

Place butter in 2-cup measure. Microwave at High 30 to 45 seconds, or until melted. Stir in flour, bouillon granules, lemon peel, chives, onion powder, salt and pepper. Blend in milk.

Reduce power to 50% (Medium). Microwave 3 to 5 minutes, or until thickened, stirring 2 or 3 times during cooking. Stir hot soup into cooked broccoli. If necessary to reheat soup for serving, microwave at 50% (Medium) 1 to 1½ minutes, or until desired temperature.

Cream of Broccoli Soup for Two: Double all ingredients. Prepare as directed except use two 15-oz. individual casseroles, dividing equally between casseroles. Microwave broccoli at High 3 to 4 minutes; butter at High 30 to 45 seconds. Reduce power to 50% (Medium). Microwave soup 3½ to 6½ minutes. Microwave to reheat, if necessary, at 50% (Medium) 2 to 2½ minutes.

Marinated ▲
Cauliflower Salad

Marinade:
¼ cup red wine vinegar
¼ cup olive oil
1 tablespoon packed brown
   sugar
1 teaspoon lemon juice
½ teaspoon dried basil leaves
¼ teaspoon salt
⅛ teaspoon pepper
¼ teaspoon dry mustard

Salad:
½ small onion, thinly sliced
½ medium green pepper, cut
   into 2 × ¼-in. strips
1 cup fresh cauliflowerets,
   page 120
1 medium tomato, cut into
   ¾-in. cubes

Makes about 2 cups

In 1-qt. casserole combine all
marinade ingredients.
Microwave at High 30 to 60
seconds, or until heated and
sugar dissolves, stirring after
half the time. Add onion, green
pepper and cauliflowerets,
tossing to coat. Cover.
Microwave at High 1½ to 2½
minutes, or until vegetables are
tender-crisp, stirring after half
the cooking time. Stir in tomato.
Refrigerate until chilled. Refrigerate no longer than 2 days.

Cauliflower With Cheese-Horseradish Sauce

½ cup fresh or frozen
   cauliflowerets, page 120
1 green onion, chopped
2 teaspoons water
1 teaspoon butter or margarine
1 teaspoon all-purpose flour
   Dash salt
   Dash white pepper
¼ cup milk
1 tablespoon shredded
   Cheddar cheese
1 teaspoon dairy sour cream
¼ teaspoon prepared
   horseradish

Serves 1

Place cauliflower, chopped onion and water in small bowl or
casserole; cover. Microwave at High 1½ to 2½ minutes, or until
cauliflower is tender-crisp, stirring once during cooking time. Drain
and set aside.

Place butter in 1-cup measure. Microwave at High 20 to 30
seconds, or until melted. Stir in flour, salt and white pepper. Blend
in milk. Microwave at High 45 to 60 seconds, or until thickened.
Stir in cheese, sour cream and horseradish, stirring until cheese
melts and sauce is smooth. Stir into hot vegetables.

Variation:
Broccoli With Cheese Sauce: Substitute ½ cup broccoli cuts for
cauliflower and Monterey Jack cheese for Cheddar cheese. Omit
horseradish. Prepare as directed.

Cauliflower or Broccoli With Sauce for Two: Double all
ingredients. Prepare as directed except microwave vegetables at
High 2½ to 3½ minutes. Place butter in 2-cup measure; microwave at High 30 to 45 seconds. Microwave sauce at High 1 to
1½ minutes.

Making the Most of Lettuce & Cabbage

Lettuce and cabbage are indispensable for fresh, green salads, but they can also be used in a variety of cooked dishes. One head makes several servings. Lettuce and cabbage cannot be frozen, but will keep several days to a week when stored properly in the refrigerator. Store them unwashed in plastic bags or covered containers.

Recipes that use a portion of 1-lb. lettuce head:
  Pineapple Chicken in Lettuce Leaves, page 88
  Garden Vegetable Soup, page 24
  Cornish Hen With Lettuce Stuffing, page 97
  Wilted Tossed Salad, page 125
  Lettuce Soup, page 125

Recipes that use a portion of 1-lb. cabbage:
  Ham-Stuffed Cabbage Rolls, page 65
  Hot Vegetable Drink, page 19
  Cabbage & Bratwurst, page 76
  Cabbage Stew With Dumplings, page 126
  Fruited Slaw, page 126

How to Prepare Lettuce

Outer leaves. If leaves are difficult to remove, place lettuce head in 2-qt. casserole; cover. Microwave at High 30 to 60 seconds, or until outer leaves are pliable enough to remove.

Shredded. Stand head upright. Slice vertically in half. Remove core. Place one half at a time flat side down. Using knuckles to guide knife, slice thinly across lettuce to shred. To chop, cut shreds crosswise.

Salad pieces. Tear, rather than cut, lettuce into pieces. Vary appearance of salad by cutting head in wedges.

How to Prepare Cabbage

Outer leaves. Microwave whole cabbage head at High 1 to 3 minutes, or until leaves can be separated easily and removed from head. To prepare for stuffing, cut out center rib.

Shredded. Stand head upright. Slice vertically in half. Remove core. Place one half at a time flat side down. Using knuckles to guide knife, slice thinly across cabbage to shred.

Chopped. Cut as for shreds, but make thicker pieces, using free hand to steady knife. Guide knife in up and down motion across shreds to chop.

Wilted Tossed Salad

Salad:
2 cups torn lettuce, opposite
1 small tomato, cut into thin
   wedges
½ cup fresh cauliflowerets,
   optional
¼ cup seasoned croutons
2 tablespoons grated carrot
2 tablespoons sliced celery
2 teaspoons grated Parmesan
   cheese

Dressing:
1 slice bacon, cut into ½-in.
   pieces
1 new potato, thinly sliced
2 teaspoons finely chopped
   onion
2 tablespoons vegetable oil
1 tablespoon cider vinegar
1 teaspoon sugar
1 teaspoon Worcestershire
   sauce
¼ teaspoon salt
⅛ teaspoon coarse ground
   black pepper

Serves 2

Combine salad ingredients in bowl. Toss. Set aside. Place bacon in small dish or casserole. Microwave at High 45 seconds to 1½ minutes, or until brown, stirring after half the time. Remove bacon from drippings; drain on paper towel. Add bacon to salad.

Stir potato and onion into bacon drippings. Microwave at High 1 to 2½ minutes, or until potato is tender, stirring after half the time. Stir in oil, vinegar, sugar, Worcestershire sauce, salt and pepper. Microwave at High 45 seconds to 1½ minutes, or until boiling. Stir. Immediately pour over salad ingredients, tossing to coat. Let stand 5 minutes until lettuce is wilted.

Wilted Tossed Salad for One:
Refrigerate one serving no longer than 2 days.

Lettuce Soup ▲

1 tablespoon thinly sliced
   celery
1 tablespoon chopped green
   pepper
1 tablespoon thinly sliced
   green onion
2 teaspoons butter or
   margarine
1 cup hot water

¾ cup shredded lettuce,
   opposite
2 tablespoons instant rice
4 thin carrot strips, thinly sliced
   with vegetable peeler
1 teaspoon instant chicken
   bouillon granules
⅛ teaspoon salt
⅛ teaspoon pepper
1 lemon slice, ⅛-in. thick

Serves 1

Place celery, green pepper, onion and butter in 15-oz. individual casserole or bowl; cover. Microwave at High 1½ to 2½ minutes, or until vegetables are tender, stirring after half the time. Stir in water, lettuce, rice, carrot, bouillon granules, salt, pepper and lemon slice; cover. Microwave at High 1½ to 2½ minutes, or until heated. Stir.

Lettuce Soup for Two: Double all ingredients. Prepare as directed except use two 15-oz. individual casseroles or bowls and divide ingredients equally between casseroles. Microwave vegetables at High 2½ to 3½ minutes; soup, 2½ to 3 minutes.

Cabbage Stew
With Dumplings

1 slice bacon, cut into pieces
1 tablespoon all-purpose flour
¼ teaspoon celery seed
⅛ teaspoon garlic powder
⅛ teaspoon pepper
½ teaspoon instant chicken
    bouillon granules
½ cup hot water
1 can (6 oz.) vegetable juice
    cocktail
1 cup shredded cabbage,
    page 124
2 new potatoes, cut into ½-in.
    cubes
1 medium tomato, peeled and
    cut into ½-in. cubes
1 medium carrot, thinly sliced
¼ cup onion, chopped

Dumplings:
⅓ cup Dry Quick Bread Mix,
    page 135
2 teaspoons snipped fresh
    parsley
2 tablespoons beer or water

Serves 2

Place bacon in 1- to 1½-qt. casserole. Microwave at High 45 to 60 seconds, or until brown. Stir in flour, celery seed, garlic powder and pepper.

In 2-cup measure dissolve bouillon granules in water. Add vegetable juice. Blend into flour mixture. Stir in cabbage, potatoes, tomato, carrot and onion; cover. Microwave at High 25 to 30 minutes, or until vegetables are tender, stirring 2 or 3 times.

In small bowl combine quick bread mix and parsley. Stir in beer just until moistened. Drop by four spoonfuls onto vegetables; cover. Microwave at High 2 to 3½ minutes, or until dumplings are light and springy to the touch, and no longer doughy.

Cabbage Stew With Dumplings for One: Refrigerate one serving no longer than 2 days. To reheat, microwave at 70% (Medium-High) 2½ to 4 minutes, stirring stew after half the time.

Fruited Slaw ▲

Dressing:
2 teaspoons butter or
    margarine
2 teaspoons all-purpose flour
1 tablespoon sugar
¼ teaspoon dry mustard
⅛ teaspoon salt
    Dash pepper
⅓ cup half and half
2 tablespoons apple juice
2 teaspoons white vinegar
1 egg yolk, beaten

Salad:
2 cups chopped cabbage,
    page 124
1 can (8 oz.) crushed
    pineapple, drained
1 can (11 oz.) mandarin
    orange sections, drained
¼ cup chopped walnuts

Serves 2

Place butter in 2-cup measure. Microwave at High 30 to 45 seconds, or until melted. Stir in flour. Blend in remaining dressing ingredients, except egg yolk. Microwave at High 1 to 2½ minutes, or until thickened, stirring every 30 seconds. Stir small amount of hot mixture into beaten egg yolk. Return to hot mixture, stirring constantly. Set aside. In medium bowl combine cabbage, pineapple, orange sections and walnuts. Stir in dressing, tossing to coat. Refrigerate until chilled, about 2 hours.

Fruited Slaw for One: Refrigerate one serving no longer than 2 days.

Artichoke ▲

1 whole fresh artichoke

Serves 1

Trim artichoke 1 inch from top and close to base so it will stand. Snap off small lower leaves and snip tips of outer leaves. Rinse; shake·off water. Brush with lemon juice to prevent discoloration. Wrap in plastic wrap, or place in 8 × 8-in. baking dish with ¼ cup water and cover with plastic wrap. Microwave at High 4 to 5 minutes, or until lower leaves can be pulled off and base pierces easily with fork. Rotate after half the time. Let stand 3 to 5 minutes.

Artichokes for Two: Use two artichokes. Prepare as directed except microwave at High 5½ to 8½ minutes, rearranging once. Let stand 3 to 5 minutes.

Artichoke Mustard Dip

½ pkg. (3 oz.) cream cheese
1 tablespoon mayonnaise or
   salad dressing
½ teaspoon Dijon-style mustard

Serves 1

Place cream cheese in small bowl or dish. Microwave at High 10 to 20 seconds, or until softened. Blend in mayonnaise and mustard. Serve with artichoke.

Variation:
Artichoke Onion Dip: Prepare as directed except omit mustard. Stir in ⅛ teaspoon onion salt and ¼ teaspoon lemon pepper.

Artichoke Dips for Two:
Double all ingredients. Prepare as directed except soften cream cheese at High 15 to 30 seconds.

Artichoke Butter Dip ▲

¼ cup butter
¼ teaspoon lemon juice

Serves 1

Place butter in small bowl. Microwave at High 45 to 60 seconds, or until melted. Stir in lemon juice. Serve with artichoke.

Variation:
Lemon-Sour Cream Dip: Add 2 tablespoons dairy sour cream to prepared dip. Beat with fork until smooth.

Artichoke Dips for Two:
Double all ingredients. Prepare as directed except microwave butter at High 45 seconds to 1¼ minutes.

Vegetables Au Gratin

- 1 new potato, peeled and thinly sliced
- 1 tablespoon chopped onion
- 1 tablespoon butter or margarine
- 2 teaspoons all-purpose flour
- ⅛ teaspoon salt
- ⅛ teaspoon paprika
  Dash pepper
- 1 tablespoon milk
- ⅓ cup sliced zucchini
- ½ medium tomato, seeds removed and chopped

Topping:
- 1½ teaspoons butter or margarine
- 1 tablespoon grated Parmesan cheese
- 1 tablespoon seasoned bread crumbs

Serves 1

Combine potato, onion and butter in 12-oz. individual casserole; cover. Microwave at High 2 to 3 minutes, or until tender, stirring after half the time. Stir in flour, salt, paprika and pepper. Blend in milk. Stir in zucchini and tomato. Microwave at High 2 to 3 minutes, or until tomato and zucchini soften, stirring 2 or 3 times.

Place butter for topping in small bowl. Microwave at High 15 to 30 seconds, or until melted. Stir in cheese and bread crumbs. Sprinkle over vegetables. Microwave at High 30 to 60 seconds, or until heated.

Vegetables Au Gratin for Two: Double all ingredients. Prepare as directed except use 15-oz. individual casserole. Microwave potato, onion and butter at High 3 to 4 minutes; remaining vegetables, 3 to 4 minutes; butter for topping, 30 to 45 seconds; vegetables with topping, 30 to 60 seconds.

Spinach Lasagna ▲

- 1 lasagna noodle, page 131
- ¼ pkg. (10 oz.) frozen chopped spinach
- ¼ cup ricotta cheese
- ¼ cup shredded mozzarella cheese, divided
- ⅛ teaspoon garlic salt
- 1 small tomato
- 1 tablespoon catsup
- 1 teaspoon finely chopped onion
  Dash pepper

Serves 1

Prepare noodle as directed. Cut noodle crosswise in half and set aside. With a serrated knife, cut off one-fourth of frozen spinach. Wrap remaining spinach and return to freezer. Place one-fourth in medium bowl; cover. Microwave at High 1 to 1½ minutes, or until defrosted, stirring to break apart after half the time. Drain, pressing out moisture. Stir in ricotta cheese, 2 tablespoons mozzarella cheese and the garlic salt. Set aside.

Cut two thin slices from tomato; set aside. Chop remaining tomato. Place chopped tomato, catsup, onion and pepper in 1-cup measure. Microwave at High 2 to 3 minutes, or until tomato and onion are tender, stirring 2 or 3 times during cooking.

In 6¾ × 4½-in. individual casserole layer one noodle half, half of spinach mixture and half of tomato mixture. Repeat once, topping with the two tomato slices. Sprinkle with remaining 2 tablespoons mozzarella cheese. Microwave at High 2 to 3 minutes, or until cheese melts and mixture is heated, rotating casserole ½ turn after half the cooking time.

Spinach Lasagna for Two: Double all ingredients. Prepare as directed except use two 6¾ × 4½-in. individual casseroles. Divide ingredients equally between casseroles. Microwave spinach at High 1½ to 2½ minutes; tomato mixture, 4 to 5 minutes; layered mixtures, 4 to 5 minutes.

Vegetable Sukiyaki

1 serving brown rice,
    page 133
1 cup fresh bean sprouts
1 small tomato, chopped
1 small carrot, cut into
    2½ × ¼-in. strips
1 green onion, sliced
    diagonally
¼ cup diagonally sliced celery
¼ cup sliced fresh mushrooms
1 teaspoon sugar
¼ teaspoon instant beef
    bouillon granules
1 tablespoon water
1 tablespoon soy sauce
1½ teaspoons sherry
½ teaspoon cornstarch

Serves 1

Prepare brown rice as directed. Set aside. In 1-qt. casserole combine bean sprouts, tomato, carrot, onion, celery and mushrooms; cover. Microwave at High 4 to 6 minutes, or until tender-crisp, stirring 2 or 3 times during cooking.

Drain any vegetable juices into 1-cup measure. Add sugar, bouillon granules, water, soy sauce and sherry. Stir in cornstarch. Microwave at High 1 to 1½ minutes, or until clear and thickened, stirring after half the time. Stir sauce. Pour over hot vegetables, mixing to coat. Serve over brown rice.

Vegetable Sukiyaki for Two:
Double all ingredients. Prepare as directed except use 2-qt. casserole. Microwave vegetables at High 6 to 9 minutes. Microwave sauce in 2-cup measure at High 1½ to 2 minutes, stirring twice.

Vegetable Enchiladas ▲

Sauce:
2 tablespoons chopped onion
2 tablespoons chopped green
    pepper
¾ cup tomato juice
3 tablespoons catsup
2 tablespoons chopped green
    chilies
1 teaspoon sugar
½ teaspoon instant beef
    bouillon granules

¼ teaspoon chili powder
⅛ teaspoon ground cumin

Enchiladas:
2 cups shredded lettuce,
    page 124
1 can (8 oz.) kidney beans,
    drained
¼ cup chopped black olives
4 corn tortillas, 6-in. diameter
½ cup shredded Cheddar
    cheese, divided

Serves 2

In 2-cup measure combine onion and green pepper. Cover with plastic wrap. Microwave at High 1½ to 2½ minutes, or until tender, stirring after half the time. Add remaining sauce ingredients. Microwave, uncovered, at High 1 to 2 minutes, or until sauce is heated and flavors blend, stirring after half the time.

In medium bowl combine lettuce, kidney beans and olives. Pour on half the sauce, tossing to coat. Place one-fourth mixture on each tortilla. Sprinkle 1 tablespoon cheese over each. Roll up.

Place seam side down in 10 × 6-in. baking dish. Pour remaining sauce evenly over filled tortillas. Sprinkle with remaining cheese. Cover with wax paper. Microwave at High 4 to 6 minutes, or until filling is heated and cheese melts, rotating casserole ½ turn after half the time. Garnish with shredded lettuce and dairy sour cream, if desired.

Vegetable Enchilada for One: Refrigerate one serving no longer than 2 days. To reheat, microwave at 70% (Medium-High) 5 to 7 minutes.

Pasta & Rice

Pasta and rice, which are popular additions to main dishes, also make tempting side dishes. Try them lightly sauced or mixed with vegetables. For a side dish, use one-half serving of pasta. A full serving makes enough for a main dish.

Linguine With Clam Sauce

1 serving linguine, opposite
2 tablespoons finely chopped onion
2 tablespoons butter or margarine
1 tablespoon olive oil
⅛ teaspoon garlic powder
1 tablespoon all-purpose flour
1 tablespoon snipped fresh parsley
¼ teaspoon salt
⅛ teaspoon pepper
1 can (6½ oz.) minced clams, drained, ⅓ cup juice reserved
2 tablespoons milk

Serves 2

Prepare linguine as directed. Cover and set aside. In 4-cup measure combine onion, butter, olive oil and garlic powder. Microwave at High 1 to 2 minutes, or until onion is tender and butter melts. Blend in flour. Stir in parsley, salt, pepper, clams, clam juice and milk. Microwave at High 1 to 3 minutes, or until thickened, stirring once or twice. Pour over hot linguine, tossing to coat. Sprinkle each serving with grated Parmesan cheese and snipped fresh parsley, if desired.

Linguine With Clam Sauce for One: Refrigerate one serving no longer than 2 days. To reheat, microwave at 70% (Medium-High) 1½ to 2½ minutes, stirring after half the time.

Vegetables & Fettuccine ▲

½ serving fettuccine, opposite
1 tablespoon butter, divided
⅛ teaspoon dried oregano leaves
½ cup fresh broccoli flowerets
¼ small onion, thinly sliced
¼ cup sliced fresh mushrooms
2 cherry tomatoes, quartered

¼ cup half and half
2 tablespoons grated Romano cheese
1 tablespoon grated Parmesan cheese
1 tablespoon ricotta or cottage cheese
¼ teaspoon salt

Serves 1

Prepare fettuccine as directed. Toss with 1½ teaspoons butter and the oregano. Set aside. In small dish combine remaining 1½ teaspoons butter, the broccoli and onion; cover. Microwave at High 1 to 2 minutes, or until tender. Stir in remaining ingredients. Add to fettuccine, tossing to coat. Place in 15-oz. individual casserole; cover. Reduce power to 50% (Medium). Microwave 3 to 4 minutes, or until heated, stirring after half the time.

Vegetables & Fettuccine for Two: Double all ingredients. Prepare as directed except microwave butter, broccoli and onion at High 2 to 4 minutes. Place all in 1-qt. casserole. Reduce power to 50% (Medium). Microwave 6 to 8 minutes.

How to Microwave Pasta

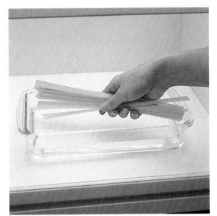

Combine water and salt in casserole as directed in chart, below. Cover with plastic wrap. Microwave 2 cups water at High 4 to 6 minutes, or 3 cups water 5 to 8 minutes, or until boiling.

Add pasta. Microwave, uncovered, at High as directed in chart, until tender but firm, stirring after half the time.

Drain and rinse pasta under running water. If used in salads or baked dishes, rinse with cold water. With sauces, use hot water. After draining, place lasagna and jumbo shells on paper towels.

Pasta Chart

½ serving is 1 oz. of pasta; 1 serving is 2 oz.; 2 servings are 4 oz.*

Pasta	Amount	Casserole Size	Water	Salt	Microwave Time
Egg Noodles Wide	½, 1 or 2 servings	2-qt. casserole	3 cups	½ tsp.	4½ - 6½ min.
Fettuccine	½, 1 or 2 servings	10 × 6-in. baking dish	3 cups	½ tsp.	4 - 6 min.
Lasagna	1 or 2 noodles	12 × 8-in. baking dish	2 cups plus ½ teaspoon olive oil	½ tsp.	6 - 9 min.
Linguine	½, 1 or 2 servings	10 × 6-in. baking dish	3 cups	¼ tsp.	6 - 8 min.
Macaroni Elbow	½, 1 or 2 servings	2-qt. casserole	2 cups	¼ tsp.	3 - 5 min.
Shells	½, 1 or 2 servings	2-qt. casserole	2 cups	¼ tsp.	6 - 8 min.
Jumbo Shells	6 shells	2-qt. casserole	3 cups	½ tsp.	9 - 11 min.
Mostaccioli	½, 1 or 2 servings	2-qt. casserole	3 cups	½ tsp.	7 - 9 min.
Spaghetti	½, 1 or 2 servings	10 × 6-in. baking dish	3 cups	½ tsp.	6 - 9 min.

*Egg Noodles: 1 oz. is ½ cup
  Fettuccine: 1 oz. is approximately 20 pieces
  Linguine: 1 oz. is approximately 40 pieces

Macaroni: 1 oz. of shells or elbow macaroni is ¼ cup
Mostaccioli: 2 oz. are ⅔ cup
Spaghetti: 1 oz. is approximately 40 pieces

Rice Ring ▲

2 servings long grain rice, opposite
⅓ cup chopped tomato, seeds removed
1 green onion, thinly sliced
1 tablespoon chopped green pepper
1 teaspoon olive oil
2 tablespoons snipped fresh parsley

Serves 2

Prepare rice as directed. Set aside. In 1-qt. casserole combine tomato, green onion, green pepper and olive oil. Microwave at High 1 to 2 minutes, or until vegetables are tender-crisp. Stir in parsley. Stir vegetable mixture into rice. Spoon rice mixture into greased 2½-cup ring mold. Press gently. Cover with wax paper. Microwave at High 2 to 3 minutes, or until heated. Invert onto serving plate.

NOTE: A 6½-in. glass skillet with a 6-oz. custard cup placed upright in the center can be substituted for the 2½-cup ring mold. Remove custard cup before inverting.

Curried Rice

pictured opposite, left

¼ cup chopped celery
2 teaspoons butter or margarine
1 cup hot water
½ cup uncooked long grain rice
¼ teaspoon curry powder
¼ teaspoon salt
¼ cup raisins

Serves 2

Place celery and butter in 1½-qt. casserole; cover. Microwave at High 45 to 60 seconds, or until celery is tender. Add remaining ingredients except raisins; cover. Microwave at High 3 minutes, or until boiling. Stir. Reduce power to 50% (Medium). Microwave 10 to 13 minutes, or until rice is tender. Stir in raisins; cover. Let stand 5 minutes.

Curried Rice for One: Wrap, label and freeze one serving no longer than 2 weeks. To defrost and heat, microwave at 70% (Medium-High) 3 to 5 minutes, stirring to break apart after half the time.

Seasoned Brown Rice

pictured opposite, middle

2 tablespoons chopped green onion
1 tablespoon chopped celery
2 teaspoons snipped fresh parsley
1½ teaspoons butter or margarine
1¾ cups hot water
½ cup uncooked brown rice
½ teaspoon instant chicken bouillon granules
¼ teaspoon salt

Serves 2

Place green onion, celery, parsley and butter in 2-qt. casserole; cover. Microwave at High 45 to 60 seconds, or until tender, stirring once. Add remaining ingredients; cover.

Microwave at High 4 minutes, or until boiling. Stir. Reduce power to 50% (Medium). Microwave 40 to 45 minutes, or until rice is tender. Let stand, covered, 5 minutes. Fluff with fork.

Seasoned Brown Rice for One: Wrap, label and freeze one serving no longer than 2 weeks. To defrost and heat, microwave at 70% (Medium-High) 3 to 5 minutes, stirring once.

Cheesy Rice

pictured opposite, right

2 servings long grain rice, opposite
¼ cup shredded Swiss or Cheddar cheese
½ teaspoon dried parsley flakes
Paprika

Serves 2

Prepare rice as directed. Stir in cheese and parsley just before standing time. Cover and let stand 5 minutes. Stir. Sprinkle with paprika.

Cheesy Rice for One: Wrap, label and freeze one serving no longer than 2 weeks. To defrost and heat, microwave at 70% (Medium-High) 3 to 5 minutes, stirring after half the time.

Rice Chart

Type/Amount of Rice	Water	Salt	Butter	Procedure
Instant 1 serving (6 table- spoons)	¼ cup plus 2 table-spoons	⅛ tsp.	½ tsp.	Combine water, salt and butter in 1-qt. casserole. Microwave at High 1¾ to 2½ minutes, or until boiling. Stir in rice. Cover. Let stand 10 minutes, or until tender. Fluff with fork before serving.
2 servings (¾ cup)	¾ cup	¼ tsp.	1 tsp.	Prepare as directed above. Use 1½-qt. casserole. Microwave 2 to 3 minutes.
Quick-Cooking 2 servings* (1 cup)	¾ cup	¼ tsp.	1 tsp.	Combine rice, water, salt and butter in 1- to 1½-qt. casserole. Cover. Microwave at High 2½ to 3½ minutes, or until rice is tender. Fluff with fork before serving.
Long Grain 2 servings* (½ cup)	1 cup	¼ tsp.	1 tsp.	Combine rice, water, salt and butter in 1½-qt. casserole. Cover. Microwave at High 3 minutes, or until boiling. Stir. Reduce power to 50% (Medium). Microwave 8 to 10 minutes, or until rice is tender. Let stand 5 minutes. Fluff with fork before serving.
Brown 2 servings* (½ cup)	1¾ cups	¼ tsp.	1½ tsp.	Combine rice, water, salt and butter in 2-qt. casserole. Cover. Microwave at High 4 minutes, or until boiling. Stir. Reduce power to 50% (Medium). Microwave 40 to 45 minutes, or until rice is tender. Let stand 5 minutes. Fluff with fork before serving.
Wild 1 serving (¼ cup)	1½ cups	¼ tsp.	—	Rinse rice under running water. Combine rice, water and salt in 2-qt. casserole. Cover. Microwave at High 20 to 30 minutes, or until kernels split, stirring every 10 minutes. Add water to cover rice, if necessary. Let stand 15 minutes. Drain before serving.
2 servings (½ cup)	3 cups	½ tsp.	—	Prepare as directed above. Use 3-qt. casserole. Microwave 30 to 40 minutes.

*If desired, wrap, label and freeze one serving no longer than 2 weeks. To defrost and heat, microwave at 70% (Medium-High) 3 to 5 minutes.

Breads

Freshly baked bread, still warm from the oven, is a treat rarely enjoyed by small households. With the recipes in this section, you can microwave a variety of miniature loaves, muffins, even a coffee cake just right for one or two.

Dry Quick Bread Mix

3½ cups all-purpose flour
  ½ cup dry buttermilk powder
  ½ cup sugar
  2 teaspoons baking powder
  2 teaspoons baking soda
  1 teaspoon salt
  ¼ cup plus 2 tablespoons
    shortening

Makes 5 cups

Sift together flour, buttermilk powder, sugar, baking powder, baking soda and salt. Cut in shortening with pastry blender. Place in airtight container. Refrigerate no longer than 4 weeks. Use in the recipes on the following pages.

Gingered ▶ Applesauce Bread

  1 cup Dry Quick Bread Mix,
    above
  ½ cup chunky applesauce
  ¼ cup raisins
  2 tablespoons chopped
    walnuts
  2 tablespoons hot water
  1 tablespoon molasses
  1 egg
  ½ teaspoon ground cinnamon
  ¼ teaspoon ground ginger

Makes 1 loaf

Line bottom of 6½ × 4-in. loaf dish with wax paper. Mix all ingredients just until moistened. Pour into prepared dish. Microwave at 50% (Medium) 7 to 12 minutes, or until light and springy to the touch and no uncooked batter remains on sides or bottom, rotating every 2 minutes. Let stand 5 to 10 minutes. Remove from dish. Wrap and refrigerate any leftover bread.

Cottage Deli Dinner Loaf

  1 cup Dry Quick Bread Mix, left
  ⅓ cup cream-style cottage
    cheese, small curd
  3 tablespoons milk
  1 egg
  1 teaspoon dried dill weed
  ¼ teaspoon onion powder
  3 tablespoons corn flake
    crumbs, divided
  2 tablespoons grated
    Parmesan cheese

Makes 1 loaf

Line bottom of 6½ × 4-in. loaf dish with wax paper. Mix quick bread mix, cottage cheese, milk, egg, dill weed, onion powder, 2 tablespoons corn flake crumbs and the Parmesan cheese just until moistened. Spread in prepared dish.

Microwave at 50% (Medium) 4 minutes, rotating ½ turn every 2 minutes. Sprinkle with remaining 1 tablespoon corn flake crumbs. Microwave at 50% (Medium) 1 to 4 minutes, or until light and springy to the touch and no uncooked batter remains on sides or bottom, rotating ¼ turn every 2 minutes. Let stand 5 minutes. Remove from dish. Wrap and refrigerate any leftover bread.

Orange Bran ▲ Refrigerator Muffins

1 cup whole bran cereal
¾ cup orange juice
⅓ cup packed dark brown
    sugar
1 egg, slightly beaten
1 teaspoon grated orange peel
1 cup Dry Quick Bread Mix,
    page 135

Makes 16 to 18 muffins

Place cereal and orange juice in medium bowl. Let stand 5 minutes, or until mixture can be stirred smooth. Mix in brown sugar, egg and orange peel. Stir in quick bread mix just until moistened. Muffin mixture can be stored in refrigerator no longer than 1 week.

To microwave muffins, line each custard cup or microwave muffin cup with two paper liners. Fill each cup half full. Microwave at High as directed in chart, below, or until light and springy to the touch, rotating ½ turn after half the time. Moist spots will dry on standing.

Amount	Microwave Time at High
1	20 - 40 seconds
2	½ - 1½ minutes
4	1 - 2½ minutes
6	1¾ - 4½ minutes

Peanut Butter Bran Muffins

pictured page 134, upper right

¼ cup whole bran cereal
¼ cup milk
1 tablespoon plus 1½
    teaspoons beaten egg
1 tablespoon honey
2 teaspoons packed brown
    sugar
2 teaspoons creamy peanut
    butter
¼ cup plus 2 tablespoons Dry
    Quick Bread Mix, page 135

Makes 6 muffins

Line each of six custard cups or microwave muffin cups with two paper liners. Place cereal and milk in small bowl. Let stand 5 minutes, or until mixture can be stirred smooth. Add egg, honey, brown sugar and peanut butter. Stir in dry quick bread mix just until moistened. Fill each cup half full.

Microwave at High 1¾ to 4½ minutes, or until light and springy to the touch, rotating ½ turn after half the time. Moist spots will dry on standing.

Peanut Butter Bran Muffins for One: Wrap, label and freeze any remaining muffins no longer than 4 weeks. To defrost and heat, microwave one muffin at High 15 to 30 seconds, or until warm to the touch.

Prune Bread ▲

1 tablespoon plus 1½
    teaspoons graham
    cracker crumbs
1 cup prunes
1⅓ cups water, divided
1 cup Dry Quick Bread Mix,
    page 135
2 tablespoons packed dark
    brown sugar
⅛ teaspoon ground nutmeg
1 egg, slightly beaten

Makes 1 loaf

Lightly grease 6½ × 4-in. loaf dish. Coat evenly with crumbs. Place prunes and 1 cup water in 1-qt. casserole; cover. Microwave at High 5 to 7 minutes, or until prunes plump, stirring after half the time. Let stand, covered, 10 to 15 minutes. Remove pits from prunes and discard. Chop pulp and set aside. In medium bowl combine quick bread mix, brown sugar and nutmeg. Blend in remaining ⅓ cup water and the egg. Stir in prunes.

Spread batter evenly in prepared loaf dish. Reduce power to 50% (Medium). Microwave 6 to 9 minutes, or until light and springy to the touch and no uncooked batter remains on sides or bottom, rotating ¼ turn every 2 minutes. Let stand on counter 5 to 10 minutes. Loosen edges and remove from dish. Wrap and refrigerate any leftover bread.

Corn Bread
pictured page 134 upper left

⅓ cup all-purpose flour
⅓ cup cornmeal
 1 teaspoon baking powder
½ teaspoon sugar
¼ teaspoon salt
¼ cup milk
 1 egg, slightly beaten
 1 tablespoon vegetable oil

Makes 1 loaf

Line 6½ × 4-in. loaf dish with wax paper. Combine flour, cornmeal, baking powder, sugar and salt in small bowl. Blend in milk, egg and oil. Pour into prepared dish.

Microwave at 50% (Medium) 2 to 4 minutes, or until light and springy to the touch and no uncooked batter remains on sides or bottom, rotating after half the time. Let stand 5 minutes. Remove from dish. Wrap and refrigerate any leftover bread.

Whole Wheat Honey Bread
pictured page 134, center

 1 cup whole wheat flour
½ teaspoon baking soda
¼ teaspoon salt
½ cup buttermilk
 1 egg, well beaten
 1 tablespoon honey
 2 tablespoons wheat germ

Makes 1 loaf

In medium bowl combine flour, baking soda and salt. In small bowl beat buttermilk, egg and honey. Stir into dry ingredients until well blended. Dough will be wet and sticky. Shape into a ball and place in 8 × 8-in. baking dish. Sprinkle with wheat germ.

Microwave at 50% (Medium) 5 to 8 minutes, or until springy but not doughy to touch, rotating every 2 minutes. Moist spots will dry on standing. Let stand 5 to 10 minutes. Serve with honey, if desired. Wrap and refrigerate any leftover bread.

Sour Cream Coffee Cake ▲

¼ cup plus 2 tablespoons
  sugar, divided
½ teaspoon ground cinnamon
¼ cup chopped nuts
 2 tablespoons butter or
  margarine
 1 egg
½ teaspoon vanilla
½ cup all-purpose flour
¼ teaspoon baking powder
¼ teaspoon baking soda
⅛ teaspoon salt
⅓ cup dairy sour cream

Makes 1 coffee cake

In small bowl combine 2 tablespoons sugar, the cinnamon and nuts. Set aside. Place butter in medium bowl. Microwave at 10% (Low) 15 to 30 seconds, or until soft. Add remaining ¼ cup sugar, the egg and vanilla. Beat until light and fluffy. Mix in flour, baking powder, baking soda, salt, and sour cream. Spread half of batter in 22-oz. individual casserole. Sprinkle with half of the cinnamon-sugar mixture. Spread with remaining batter. Sprinkle with remaining cinnamon-sugar mixture. Increase power to 50% (Medium). Microwave 4 to 6 minutes, or until light and springy to the touch, rotating every 2 minutes. Let stand 5 minutes. Wrap and refrigerate any leftover coffee cake.

Sauces & Gravies

◄ Brown Gravy

1 tablespoon butter or meat drippings
1 tablespoon all-purpose flour
½ teaspoon instant beef bouillon granules
Dash pepper
½ cup hot water
⅛ teaspoon bouquet sauce

Makes ½ cup

Place butter in 2-cup measure. Microwave at High 30 to 45 seconds, or until melted. Blend in flour, bouillon granules and pepper. Gradually stir in water. Mix in bouquet sauce. Microwave at High 1 to 1½ minutes, or until thickened, stirring every 30 seconds. Refrigerate no longer than 2 days. To reheat, microwave at High 30 to 60 seconds, stirring once.

Mushroom Sauce

1 tablespoon butter or margarine
1 tablespoon plus 1 teaspoon all-purpose flour
½ cup hot water
½ cup sliced fresh mushrooms
½ teaspoon instant beef bouillon granules
¼ teaspoon onion powder
⅛ teaspoon Worcestershire sauce
⅛ teaspoon bouquet sauce

Makes ⅔ cup

Place butter in 2-cup measure. Microwave at High 30 to 45 seconds, or until melted. Blend in flour. Stir in remaining ingredients. Microwave at High 2½ to 3½ minutes, or until thickened, stirring after each minute. Refrigerate no longer than 2 days. To reheat, microwave at High 30 to 60 seconds, stirring once.

White Sauce ▲

  1 tablespoon butter or
    margarine
  1 tablespoon all-purpose flour
⅛ teaspoon salt
    Dash pepper
½ cup milk

Makes ½ cup

Place butter in 2-cup measure.
Microwave at High 30 to 45
seconds, or until melted. Stir in
flour, salt and pepper. Blend in
milk. Microwave at High 1 to 2
minutes, or until thickened,
stirring every 30 seconds.
Refrigerate no longer than 2
days. To reheat, microwave at
70% (Medium-High) 45 seconds
to 1½ minutes, stirring once.

Variations:
Cheese Sauce: Stir 2
tablespoons shredded Cheddar
cheese into prepared White
Sauce until melted.

Mornay Sauce: Blend 2
teaspoons grated Parmesan
cheese, 2 tablespoons
shredded Swiss cheese and ¼
teaspoon dried parsley flakes
into prepared White Sauce until
cheese melts.

Raisin Sauce ►

¼ cup packed brown sugar
  2 teaspoons cornstarch
⅛ teaspoon ground cinnamon
⅛ teaspoon dry mustard
    Dash ground cloves
½ cup apple juice
¼ cup raisins
  1 teaspoon butter or margarine

Makes ¾ cup

In 2-cup measure mix brown
sugar, cornstarch, cinnamon,
dry mustard and cloves. Mix in
apple juice. Microwave at High
1½ to 3 minutes, or until clear
and thickened, stirring every 30
seconds. Stir in raisins and
butter until butter melts. Serve
with ham or pork roast. Refrigerate no longer than 2 days. To
reheat, microwave at High 30 to
60 seconds, stirring once.

Variation:
Raisin Dessert Sauce: Prepare
as directed except omit dry
mustard. Serve over ice cream
or pound cake.

Dessert Toppings

These almost-instant dessert toppings make just one or two servings. Sweet and fruity, they add extra flavor to cakes and ice cream.

◄ Caramel Dessert Topping

6 caramels
1 tablespoon half and half

Serves 1

Place caramels and half and half in 2-cup measure. Microwave at 50% (Medium) 1½ to 2 minutes, or until caramels melt, stirring every 30 seconds. Serve over ice cream or cake.

Variation:

Caramel Banana Sauce: Prepare as directed except use 1½ teaspoons creme de banana liqueur and 1½ teaspoons half and half. Serve over ice cream and sliced banana.

Caramel Dessert Toppings for Two: Double all ingredients. Prepare as directed except microwave at 50% (Medium) 2 to 2½ minutes.

Chocolate Sauce

1 bar (1.05 oz.) milk chocolate candy
2 teaspoons milk or half and half

Serves 1

Break up chocolate bar. Place in 2-cup measure. Add milk. Microwave at 50% (Medium) 45 to 60 seconds, or until chocolate is softened. Stir to blend. Serve over ice cream.

Variation:

Chocolate Mint Sauce: Add 1 or 2 drops peppermint extract to prepared Chocolate Sauce.

Strawberry Daiquiri ▲ Sundae Topping

1 pkg. (10 oz.) frozen sweetened strawberries
1 tablespoon cornstarch or arrowroot
⅛ teaspoon lemon peel
2 tablespoons light rum

Makes 1½ cups

Remove frozen strawberries from package. Place in medium bowl. Microwave at High 2 to 3 minutes, or until defrosted, breaking apart with a fork after half the time. If icy portions remain, let stand to complete defrosting. Remove ¼ cup juice. Blend with cornstarch; stir into strawberries with lemon peel. Microwave at High 3 to 4 minutes, or until clear and thickened, stirring after every minute. Blend in rum. Serve over ice cream. Refrigerate no longer than 2 weeks.

Hot Fudge Sauce

1 square (1 oz.) unsweetened chocolate
1 can (5⅓ oz.) evaporated milk
¾ cup sugar
½ teaspoon vanilla

Makes 1 cup

Place chocolate in large bowl. Microwave at High 1½ to 2 minutes, or until melted. Stir until smooth. Gradually add milk, beating with wire whip after each addition. Stir in sugar. Microwave at High 6 to 10 minutes, or until thickened, beating with wire whip every 2 minutes. Mix in vanilla. Serve over ice cream and bananas or brownies. Refrigerate no longer than 2 weeks.

Desserts

These small size recipes allow you to enjoy dessert without having to serve the same one day after day due to excessive leftovers. Recipes for baked desserts are often difficult to divide. Direct ingredient divisions may result in awkward measurements and alter the baking. Keep in mind that the smaller container size is particularly important for these small recipes.

◄ Blueberry-Raspberry Pie

    1 microwaved 7-in. pie shell,
      page 144
    2 cups frozen blueberries
    1 cup frozen raspberries
½ cup sugar
    3 tablespoons all-purpose flour
¼ teaspoon ground cinnamon

Makes 7-in. pie

Prepare pie shell as directed. In medium bowl combine blue-berries and raspberries. Micro-wave at High 2½ to 5 minutes, or until defrosted, stirring after half the cooking time. Stir in sugar, flour and cinnamon.

Microwave at High 3 to 4½ minutes, or until mixture begins to thicken, stirring 2 or 3 times during cooking. Pour into prepared pie shell. Microwave at High 45 to 60 seconds, or until set, rotating ½ turn after half the cooking time. Refrigerate no longer than 2 days.

◄ One Crust Pastry Shell

¼ cup shortening
¾ cup all-purpose flour
¼ teaspoon salt
2 to 4 tablespoons ice water
2 drops yellow food coloring

Makes 7-in. pie shell

Cut shortening into flour and salt using pastry blender until particles are size of small peas. Combine water and food coloring; sprinkle over flour mixture, tossing lightly with fork until particles are just moist enough to cling together and form a ball.

Flatten ball on floured pastry cloth. Roll out to ⅛-in. thick circle, at least 2 inches larger than inverted pie plate. Fit loosely into 7-in. pie plate, being careful not to stretch dough or it will shrink while microwaving. Let stand 10 minutes. Trim pastry overhang to generous ½ inch. Fold to form high-standing rim; flute. Prick with fork, continuously at bend and ½ inch apart on bottom and side.

Microwave at High 2 to 4 minutes, or until dry and opaque, rotating twice during cooking. Cool before filling.

Banana Coconut ▲ Cream Pie

1 microwaved 7-in. pie shell, left
⅓ cup sugar
2 tablespoons cornstarch
⅛ teaspoon salt
1 cup milk
2 egg yolks, slightly beaten
½ teaspoon vanilla
1 medium banana, sliced
½ cup flaked coconut, divided

Makes 7-in. pie

Prepare pie shell as directed. In medium bowl mix sugar, cornstarch and salt. Blend in milk. Microwave at High 3 to 5 minutes, or until thickened, stirring every minute. Stir a small amount of hot mixture into beaten egg yolks. Return to hot mixture, stirring constantly. Microwave at High 30 to 60 seconds, or until bubbly. Blend in vanilla. Cool 5 minutes.

On medium plate spread ¼ cup coconut. Reduce power to 70% (Medium-High). Microwave 2 to 4 minutes, or until light brown, stirring after every 30 seconds. Cool. Slice banana; place slices on bottom and side of prepared pie shell. Fold remaining ¼ cup coconut into filling. Pour into shell. Sprinkle with toasted coconut. Refrigerate 2 hours, or until set, but no longer than 1 day.

Chocolate Cheese Pie ▶

Crust:

1 microwaved 7-in. graham
   cracker crust, below

Filling:

¼ cup plus 1 tablespoon
   Kirsch, divided
2 oz. semi-sweet chocolate
1 pkg. (8 oz.) cream cheese
½ cup sugar
2 eggs

Topping:

¼ cup dairy sour cream
1 tablespoon powdered sugar
2 teaspoons Kirsch

Makes 7-in. pie

Prepare graham cracker crust
as directed. In small bowl
combine 1 tablespoon liqueur
and the chocolate. Microwave
at High 45 seconds to 1¼
minutes, or until chocolate
melts, stirring once or twice. In
medium bowl blend remaining
filling ingredients with electric
mixer. Add chocolate mixture,
beating until blended. Pour into
prepared crust. Reduce power
to 30% (Medium-Low).
Microwave 12 to 16 minutes, or
until set, rotating ½ turn 2 or 3
times. Cool.

Blend all topping ingredients in
small bowl. Spread evenly over
cooled pie. Refrigerate until
chilled. Garnish with maraschino
cherries, if desired. Refrigerate
no longer than 2 days.

Graham Cracker Crust

3 tablespoons butter or
   margarine
¾ cup graham cracker crumbs
1 tablespoon sugar

Makes one 7-in. pie crust

Place butter in 7-in. pie plate.
Microwave at High 30 to 45
seconds, or until melted. Stir in
crumbs and sugar.

Press crumbs firmly and evenly
against bottom and side of
plate. Microwave at High 45
seconds to 1½ minutes, or until
hot, rotating after half the time.
Cool before filling.

Making the Most of a Cake

One 9-oz. package of cake mix makes three different desserts. Since the Raspberry Trifle must be refrigerated for 24 hours, prepare it at the same time as the Boston Cream Pie and have it ready for the following day. Crumb Topping can be frozen or stored in an airtight container.

Recipes using Yellow Cake:
  Boston Cream Pie, below
  Raspberry Trifle, below
  Crumb Topping, below
  Stuffed Baked Apple, page 151

Yellow Cake

1 pkg. (9 oz.) yellow cake mix

Makes 9-in. cake

Prepare batter as directed on package. Pour into wax paper-lined 9-in. round baking dish. Microwave at 50% (Medium) 6 minutes, rotating ¼ turn every 3 minutes. Increase power to High. Microwave 1 to 3 minutes, or until wooden pick inserted in center comes out clean. Let stand directly on counter 5 to 10 minutes. Remove to plate. Moist spots will dry on standing. Cool.

How to Divide Yellow Cake

Invert a 10-oz. custard cup in center of microwaved cake; cut around edge to form inner circle for Boston Cream Pie, below.

Divide outer ring in half; use one half to prepare Raspberry Trifle and remaining half for Crumb Topping, below.

Boston Cream Pie
pictured opposite, bottom

Inner circle of Yellow
  Cake, above
Vanilla Cream, page 148
2 tablespoons chocolate chips
1 tablespoon light corn syrup
1 tablespoon butter or
  margarine

Serves 2

Cut cooled cake circle horizontally to make two thin layers. Spread bottom layer with Vanilla Cream. Top with second layer.

In small bowl, combine chocolate chips, corn syrup and butter. Microwave at High 1 to 1¼ minutes, or until chips are melted, stirring after half the time. Stir until smooth and glossy. Spread over top of cake. Refrigerate until served. Garnish with maraschino cherries, if desired.

Raspberry Trifle
pictured opposite, middle

¼ cup raspberry jam
1 tablespoon brandy
½ of outer ring of Yellow Cake,
  above
Vanilla Cream, page 148
1 tablespoon sliced almonds

Serves 2

In small bowl mix raspberry jam and brandy. Cut cake into ½- to ¾-in. slices. In bottom of 2-cup serving bowl layer one-third of the cake slices. Spread half of jam mixture over top. Layer another one-third cake slices. Spread with remaining jam mixture. Top with remaining cake slices. Spread evenly with Vanilla Cream. Sprinkle with almonds. Cover and refrigerate 24 hours before serving.

Crumb Topping
pictured opposite, top

½ of outer ring of Yellow Cake,
  above
⅓ cup flaked coconut
¼ cup sliced almonds
½ teaspoon ground cinnamon

Makes about 1½ cups

Crumble cake into medium bowl. Microwave at High 2 to 2½ minutes, or until crumbs are very hot, stirring every 30 seconds. Spread on wax paper to cool. (Crumbs should be dry.) Spread coconut in pie plate. Reduce power to 70% (Medium-High). Microwave 2½ to 5 minutes, or until light brown, stirring every 30 seconds. Set aside to cool. Mix crumbs, coconut, almonds and cinnamon. Store in airtight container no longer than 2 weeks. Or freeze in plastic freezer bag no longer than 4 weeks. Serve on puddings or ice cream.

146

Strawberry Shortcake ▲

1 pint fresh strawberries, hulled
   and sliced, divided
1 tablespoon sugar
¾ cup Dry Quick Bread Mix,
   page 135
¼ cup milk

¼ teaspoon grated lemon peel
¼ teaspoon vanilla
   Sweetened Whipped Cream,
   page 151

Serves 2

In small bowl mash ½ cup of the strawberries. Sprinkle sugar over
remaining berries; toss to coat. Set aside.

In small bowl mix quick bread mix, milk, lemon peel and vanilla.
Divide evenly between two 6-oz. custard cups. Microwave at High
1½ to 2 minutes, or until tops spring back when lightly touched
and no unbaked batter remains on bottom, rotating and
rearranging cups after half the time.

Loosen edges and remove shortcakes; cut in half. Combine
mashed and sliced strawberries. Fill and top shortcakes with
strawberries and whipped cream.

Vanilla Cream

2 tablespoons sugar
1 tablespoon cornstarch
   Dash salt
½ cup milk
1 egg yolk, beaten
1½ teaspoons butter or
   margarine
½ teaspoon vanilla

Makes 1 serving

In 4-cup measure or medium
bowl mix sugar, cornstarch and
salt. Gradually stir in milk.
Microwave at High 2 to 2½
minutes, or until very thick,
stirring every minute. Mix a
small amount of hot mixture into
beaten egg yolk. Return to hot
mixture, stirring constantly.
Microwave at High 30 seconds.
Stir in butter and vanilla. Cool.
Serve sprinkled with crumb
topping or as filling for other
recipes in this section.

Chocolate Zucchini ► Nut Cake

1 cup all-purpose flour
¾ cup sugar
2 tablespoons cocoa
¾ teaspoon baking powder
¼ teaspoon salt
¼ cup buttermilk
¼ cup vegetable oil
¼ cup butter or margarine
1 egg
½ teaspoon vanilla
1 cup shredded zucchini
½ cup chocolate chips
¼ cup chopped walnuts or
    pecans
    Chocolate Frosting, below

Makes 8 × 8-in. cake

Place all ingredients except Chocolate Frosting in medium bowl. Blend at low speed of electric mixer, scraping bowl constantly. Beat at medium speed 2 minutes, scraping bowl occasionally. Pour into 8 × 8-in. baking dish. Place in oven on inverted saucer. Microwave at 50% (Medium) 6 minutes, rotating ½ turn after half the time.

Increase power to High. Microwave 3½ to 6 minutes, or until wooden pick inserted in center comes out clean and no uncooked batter remains on bottom of dish. Moist spots on top will dry after standing. Let stand directly on counter to cool. Spread Chocolate Frosting on cooled cake.

Chocolate Frosting

1½ cups powdered sugar
2 tablespoons cocoa
2 tablespoons butter or
    margarine, softened
    Dash salt
½ teaspoon vanilla
2 tablespoons half and half

Frosts 8 × 8-in. cake

Beat all ingredients until smooth.

Carrot Bars

¾ cup all-purpose flour
½ cup packed brown sugar
1 teaspoon ground cinnamon
1 teaspoon ground allspice
½ teaspoon baking soda
¼ teaspoon salt

1 cup shredded carrots
¼ cup butter or margarine
2 eggs
    Cream Cheese Frosting,
    below

Makes 15 bars

In medium bowl combine all ingredients except Cream Cheese Frosting. Blend at low speed of electric mixer, scraping bowl constantly. Beat at medium speed 2 minutes, scraping bowl occasionally. Pour into 10 × 6-in. baking dish. Place in oven on inverted saucer. Microwave at 50% (Medium) 6 minutes, rotating after half the time. Increase power to High. Microwave 2½ to 4½ minutes, or until wooden pick inserted in center comes out clean and no uncooked batter remains on bottom of dish. Let stand directly on counter to cool. Spread with Cream Cheese Frosting.

Cream Cheese Frosting

1 pkg. (3 oz.) cream cheese
1 tablespoon butter or
    margarine
1½ to 2 cups powdered sugar

Dash salt
¼ cup chopped walnuts,
    optional
¼ cup raisins, optional

Frosts 10 × 6-in. cake

Place cream cheese and butter in small bowl. Microwave at 50% (Medium) 30 to 60 seconds, or until softened. Blend in sugar and salt until desired consistency. Stir in nuts and raisins. If desired, remove about 3 tablespoons frosting before adding nuts and raisins. Tint 1 tablespoon green and the remaining orange. Using a pastry tube shape carrots on top of frosted bars.

149

Orange Tarts

Filling:
    Vanilla Cream, page 148

Pastry:
  2 tablespoons plus 1½
     teaspoons butter or
     margarine
  ½ cup all-purpose flour
     Dash salt
  2 to 3 tablespoons ice water
  2 drops yellow food coloring

Glaze:
1½ teaspoons sugar
  ½ teaspoon cornstarch
  2 tablespoons water
  2 drops yellow food coloring

  1 medium orange

Serves 2

How to Microwave Orange Tarts

Prepare and cool Vanilla Cream. Set aside. Cut butter into flour and salt until particles are size of small peas. Mix water and food coloring; sprinkle by teaspoonfuls over pastry mixture, tossing lightly with fork, until particles are just moist enough to form a ball.

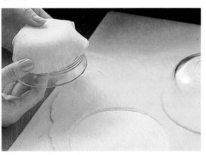

Flatten ball on floured pastry cloth. Roll out to ⅛-in. thick circle. Cut two 4½-in. circles using inverted 10-oz. custard cup as a guide. Form each circle over inverted 6-oz. custard cup. Crimp if desired.

Prick pastry shell generously. Microwave at High 2 to 3 minutes, or until dry and flaky, rotating and rearranging after each minute. Immediately remove from custard cup to wire rack. Cool.

Mix sugar, cornstarch and water for glaze in 1-cup measure. Microwave at High 45 to 60 seconds, or until clear and thickened. Stir in food coloring.

Peel orange, removing all membrane and dividing into segments. Set out cooled Vanilla Cream.

Assemble tarts by filling each pastry shell with half the Vanilla Cream. Arrange orange segments on top. Spoon glaze over oranges. Garnish with fresh mint leaves, if desired. Chill until set.

150

Bread Pudding ▶

¾ cup half and half
1 egg
3 tablespoons packed dark
    brown sugar
⅛ teaspoon ground cinnamon
⅛ teaspoon ground nutmeg
    Dash salt
1¾ cups soft bread cubes,
    ½-in. cubes*
¼ cup currants or chopped
    dates
    Brandy Sauce, below,
    optional
    Sweetened Whipped
    Cream, right, optional

Serves 2

In small bowl blend half and half, egg, brown sugar, cinnamon, nutmeg and salt. Stir in bread cubes and currants. Pour into 15-oz. individual casserole. Microwave at 50% (Medium) 6 to 10 minutes, or until center is set. Let stand 3 to 5 minutes. Pour Brandy Sauce over. Top servings with whipped cream.

*Use all white bread cubes or ¾ cup whole wheat and 1 cup white bread cubes.

Bread Pudding for One:
Refrigerate one serving no longer than 1 day. To reheat, microwave at High 1 to 1½ minutes. Top with Sweetened Whipped Cream.

Brandy Sauce

2 tablespoons packed brown
    sugar
1 tablespoon butter or
    margarine
1 tablespoon brandy

Makes about ¼ cup

In small bowl, combine brown sugar and butter. Microwave at High 30 to 60 seconds, or until bubbly, stirring once or twice. Stir in brandy. Microwave at High 30 to 60 seconds, or until smooth, stirring once.

Stuffed Baked Apple

1 large baking apple
2 tablespoons Crumb
    Topping page 146, or
    sugar cookie crumbs
1 tablespoon chopped
    pecans
    Dash ground cinnamon
2 tablespoons apple cider
1½ teaspoons sugar
    Sweetened Whipped
    Cream, right

Serves 1

Core apple, removing 1 inch from center. Place apple in 10-oz. custard cup. Chop any edible portion from core. In small bowl combine crumb topping, pecans, cinnamon and chopped apple. Spoon into apple cavity.

In 1-cup measure combine cider and sugar. Microwave at High 30 to 45 seconds, or until boiling. Pour over apple. Cover with plastic wrap. Microwave at High 1½ to 2½ minutes, or until fork tender, rotating after half the time. Let stand 2 minutes. Garnish with whipped cream. Sprinkle with additional cinnamon, if desired.

Stuffed Baked Apples for Two: Double all ingredients. Prepare as directed except microwave cider and sugar at High 45 to 60 seconds. Microwave apples 2½ to 4½ minutes, rearranging after half the time.

Sweetened Whipped Cream

½ cup chilled whipping cream
1 teaspoon sugar
¼ teaspoon vanilla

Makes 1 cup

In small chilled bowl beat whipping cream and sugar at high speed of electric mixer until soft peaks form. If desired, beat in one of the additional flavorings, below.

Variations:
Cinnamon Coffee Whipped Cream: Add 1 teaspoon coffee flavored liqueur and ⅛ teaspoon ground nutmeg.

Brandy Whipped Cream: Add 1 teaspoon brandy and ⅛ teaspoon ground nutmeg.

Cherry-Almond Whipped Cream: Add 1 teaspoon Kirsch and ¼ teaspoon almond extract.

Orange Coffee Whipped Cream: Add 1 teaspoon coffee liqueur and ⅛ teaspoon grated orange peel.

Spicy Whipped Cream: Add ⅛ teaspoon ground cinnamon, ⅛ teaspoon ground nutmeg and a dash ground cloves.

NOTE: If desired, freeze Sweetened Whipped Cream in 2-tablespoonful mounds on wax paper. When frozen, transfer to plastic bag for storage. Freeze no longer than 3 months.

Brandy Alexander Cream

2 tablespoons sugar
2 teaspoons cornstarch
1 cup chilled whipping cream, divided
½ square (1 oz.) semi-sweet chocolate
1 teaspoon dark crème de cacao liqueur
2 teaspoons brandy
1 tablespoon chopped filberts, optional

Serves 2

In 1-qt. casserole combine sugar and cornstarch. Blend in ½ cup whipping cream. Add chocolate and liqueur. Microwave at 50% (Medium) 2 to 3 minutes, or until very thick, stirring to melt chocolate every 30 seconds. Refrigerate 1 hour, or until chilled.

Beat brandy and remaining whipping cream in chilled bowl until soft peaks form. Fold into chilled chocolate mixture. Pour into two 6-oz. serving bowls. Sprinkle with filberts. Refrigerate before serving.

Spiced Prune Whip

1 cup pitted dried prunes
¾ cup port wine
½ cup water
1 stick cinnamon
2 tablespoons sugar
½ cup chilled whipping cream

Serves 2

In 1-qt. casserole combine prunes, wine, water, cinnamon and sugar. Microwave at High 10 to 13 minutes, or until prunes are tender, stirring every 3 minutes. Let stand, covered, until cool. Chill.

Drain prunes; chop. In chilled bowl, beat whipping cream until soft peaks form. Fold in prunes. Spoon into serving bowls. Refrigerate.

NOTE: Add additional ½ teaspoon port wine when beating whipping cream, if desired.

Glazed Orange ▲

1 large orange
½ teaspoon cornstarch
2 tablespoons hot water
¾ teaspoon honey
½ teaspoon orange liqueur

Serves 1

With sharp knife, cut long strip (or zest) from orange peel. Grate enough peel to measure ⅛ teaspoon. Cut remaining peel and white membrane from orange. Discard. Place orange in 10-oz. custard cup or individual serving dish. Garnish with orange peel strip.

Place cornstarch in small bowl. Stir in water, honey, liqueur and grated orange peel. Microwave at High 30 to 60 seconds, or until clear and thickened, stirring after half the time. Pour over orange. Microwave at High 1 to 1½ minutes, or until orange is heated, rotating after half the time.

Glazed Oranges for Two: Double all ingredients. Prepare as directed, except microwave sauce 1 to 2 minutes and oranges with thickened sauce 1 to 2 minutes, rearranging after half the time.

Tropical Sundae Sauce ►

1 tablespoon butter or
   margarine
¼ cup packed brown sugar
¼ cup rum
1 medium peach or pear,
   halved and sliced
4 to 6 maraschino cherries,
   halved
1 medium banana, cut into
   ½-in. pieces
   Vanilla ice cream

Serves 2

Place butter in medium bowl.
Microwave at High 30 to 45
seconds, or until melted. Stir in
brown sugar and rum until
sugar dissolves. Add peach
and cherries. Microwave at
High 1 to 2 minutes, or until
bubbly. Stir in banana. Serve
over vanilla ice cream.
Refrigerate leftover sauce no
longer than 2 days.

Rocky Road Fondue

½ cup milk chocolate chips
2 tablespoons half and half
3 large marshmallows
2 tablespoons chopped
   peanuts
¼ teaspoon vanilla
   Banana chunks, apple
   wedges, cherries, or angel
   food or pound cake cubes

Serves 1

In 2-cup measure or medium
bowl combine chocolate chips
and half and half. Microwave at
High 30 to 60 seconds, or until
chips are softened but not
melted. Add marshmallows.
Microwave at High 30 to 60
seconds, or until smooth, stirring
every 30 seconds. Stir in
peanuts and vanilla. Dip fruit or
cake into fondue with fondue
forks or wooden skewers.

Rocky Road Fondue for Two:
Double all ingredients. Prepare
as directed except microwave
chips at High 1 minute.

Index